372.8 Hawkinson, John,
H   1912-.
c.3   Rhythms, music, and
          instruments to make

372.8
H
c.3 Hawkinson, John
AUTHOR
Rhymes, Music And
TITLE
Instruments To Make

DATE DUE	BORROWER'S NAME	
2201	Jamal	306
10/1/01	Matos	215

JOHN HAWKINSON and MARTHA FAULHABER

RHYTHMS, MUSIC AND INSTRUMENTS TO MAKE

Music Involvement Series   Book Two

Illustrated by JOHN HAWKINSON

ALBERT WHITMAN & Company, Chicago

Standard Book Number 8075-6958-5 Library of Congress Card Number 70-91737
©Copyright 1970 by Albert Whitman & Company, Chicago
Published simultaneously in Canada by George J. McLeod, Limited, Toronto
Lithographed in the United States of America

372.8
M
c.3

Contents

Before You Begin...

This book is designed to show you how to explore music through your own experiments with rhythm, sound, and instruments you can make. It continues the approach of the first book in this series, **Music and Instruments for Children to Make,** a book planned for younger girls and boys.

Step-by-step instructions show how to make instruments of musical quality that belong to the three families of percussion, wind, and stringed instruments. Here are drums and other rhythm makers, xylophones, metallophones, panpipes, harps, guitars, and other stringed instruments. Each is inexpensive to build and needs only the tools found in most homes. Directions for tuning are given, and the player is urged to adjust his instrument carefully and experiment if necessary to obtain the correct sound.

For each instrument you make there are instructions for playing and examples of music. When you have several instruments, you can invite others to join you in making music. Throughout this book there are materials for different combinations of instruments and for songs to accompany. You are especially invited to invent melodies and rhythms of your own.

The pitches available on your instruments are given their letter names, A, B, C, D, E, F, G. These letter names are combined with simple rhythmic notation to help you in your playing. The rhythmic notation is explained as it is introduced and requires no previous background. All these materials can, of course, be used with standard instruments, and the choral work can be done with whatever rhythm instruments are at hand.

Anyone, young or old, can begin to learn music on his own here.

Discovering Rhythms

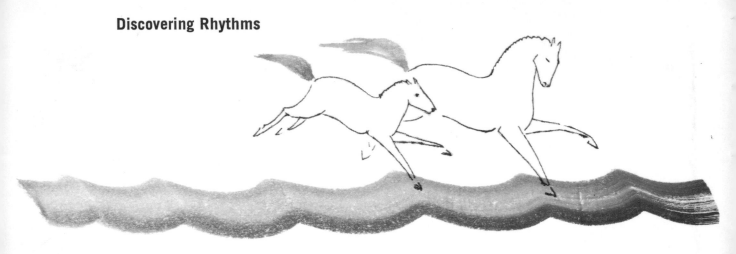

Rhythm is all around us: in the steady fall of rain,
the gallop of a horse, and the rise and fall of waves.

You can make rhythm when you walk or run or skip.
You can make rhythm when you clap or tap a drum.

6

Rhythm in Speech

There is rhythm in speech.
Clap the rhythm of each rhyme as you speak the rhyme. Give each syllable a clap. Notice the rhythmic pattern each rhyme contains.

She sells sea - shells by the sea - shore.

Pe - ter Pi - per picked a peck of pick - led pep - pers;
A peck of pick - led pep - pers Pe - ter Pi - per picked.
If Pe - ter Pi - per picked a peck of pick - led pep - pers,
Where's the peck of pick - led pep - pers Pe - ter Pi - per picked?

Oh, the grand old Duke of York,
He had ten thou - sand men.
He marched them up to the top of a hill,
And he marched them down a - gain.

And when they were up, they were up,
And when they were down, they were down,
And when they were on - ly half - way up,
They were nei - ther up nor down.

7

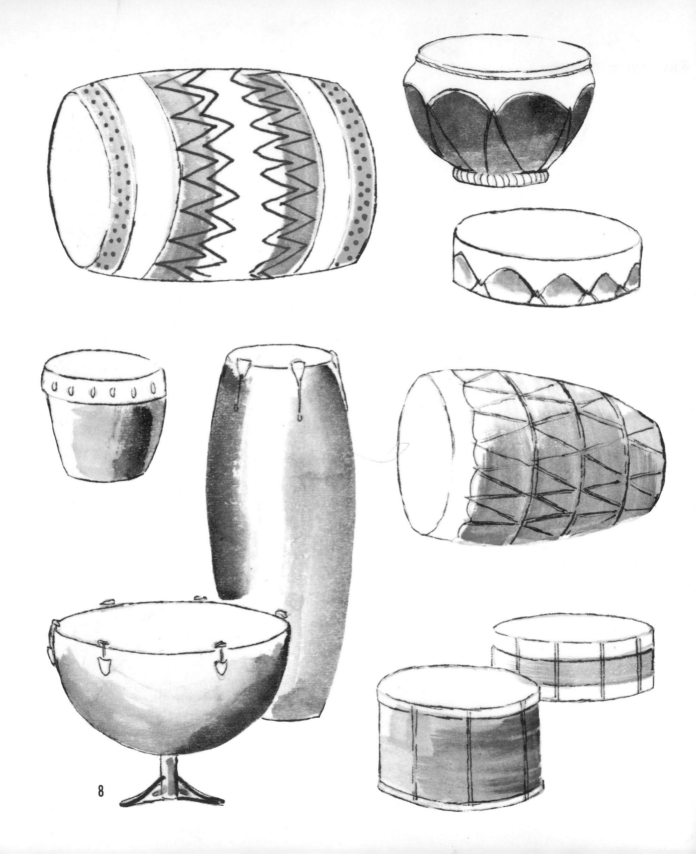

8

Drums

It is fun to tap your rhythms on an instrument. Drums have always been used for this purpose. Here are pictures of different drums that come from many lands.

Making Drums of Different Sizes

Materials you will need for making a drumhead:
1. Acetate sheathing, a dress lining fabric sold where yard goods are carried. It is best to use the heavyweight quality. One yard will make several drumheads.
2. White glue, sold in hardware or variety stores.
3. Paintbrush, 1- or 2-inch width, 3/4-inch wire nails.
4. Four or more strong wide rubber bands or cord.

For a drum cylinder you can choose a cardboard pail used for mixing paints or an empty ice cream container (from an ice cream store). Any large size cardboard container that is cylindrical makes a good bass drum. Laundry soap and some foods are stored in these containers and when empty they are usually thrown out by stores and restaurants.

A drum body can be made from 1/8-inch plywood. Cut a strip about 6 inches wide and 2 to 3 feet long. Soak in water for about 6 hours until the plywood bends easily. Make a cylinder by bending the plywood to overlap about 2 inches. Glue and nail, using a small, 3/4-inch wire nail. The nails will come through to the inside and you can use a pliers to bend over the points. Put a weight on the outside and clinch the wire nails with a hammer on the inside.

Both ends of the cylinder can be covered. This makes an excellent drum with a very full sound.

Note: Pieces of plywood 3 or 4 inches wide and about 4 feet long are considered scrap in lumberyards and can be purchased cheaply. You can use 1/4-inch plywood, but it must be soaked overnight to make it pliable. Either 1/8-inch or 1/4-inch plywood will bend more easily if the grain looks like this:

Covering the Drum

Covering the drum:

1 Cut acetate cloth about 3 inches bigger than the circumference of your drum cylinder. Place the acetate over the open drum.

2 Apply glue with a wide brush to the top of the drum and put the cloth on, as illustrated.

3 Stretch three or four rubber bands around the drum to hold the cloth in place. The bands must fit tightly. Pull the cloth out to stretch it and make it free of wrinkles.

4 Decorate the cloth with watercolors or felt pens. Round areas are interesting to decorate. You can begin at the center and work outward on one drum and do the opposite on the next drum.

5 In a small jar or pan, mix a little water with white glue. Use two parts of glue to one part of water. Apply the thinned glue to the drumhead using nice long even brushstrokes. Let the glue dry and then test the sound with a stick or the eraser end of a pencil. Additional coats of glue will give a better tone.

Rhythms for Drums

Here is a way to begin making rhythms on your drum. First, walk around the room. As you are walking, tap the drum in rhythm to your walk. Change your walking rhythm to a march by giving a heavy tap on the first walk then follow with three light taps.

Walk, walk walk walk

Try a running rhythm on your drum. As you take each step, give two short even taps, like the ticking of a clock, on your drum. The first running tap is made as you step. The second tap will fall in between your first and second step.

W a l k w a l k w a l k w a l k
Run run run run run run run run

Now tap on your drum from a walking rhythm to a running rhythm and back again to a walk.

More Rhythms for Drums

Here is another rhythm to try on your drums. You can sit down to try it out. The "walk" means give a walking tap; "run, run" means give two short even taps in place of one walking tap. You can shake your hand to the side on the "hold" if you like. Say the words as you tap.

<u>**Walk**</u> walk walk

<u>**Walk**</u> hold walk

<u>**Run**</u> run run run run run

<u>**Run**</u> run run run run run

<u>**Walk**</u> walk walk

<u>**Walk**</u> hold walk

Give a heavy tap or accent when the walk or run is underlined.

Begin a walking rhythm and have a friend join you. Let him tap a running rhythm. Listen to how the two rhythms fit together.

Drummer 1 <u>**Walk**</u> walk walk walk

Drummer 2 <u>**Run**</u> run run run run run run run

Here is another pattern to try.

Drummer 1 <u>**Walk**</u> walk run run walk

Drummer 2 <u>**Run**</u> run run run walk walk

In music, the walking tap is called a quarter note. When the walking tap divides into two running taps, each is called an eighth note. A "walk-hold" is called a half note.

Setting Up Rhythmic Patterns for Your Drums

Rhythms sometimes fall into regular patterns of pulses or beats. Tap a walking rhythm in patterns of two. Tap the first "walk" with a heavy accent as shown by the underline, tap the second "walk" lightly. The line between each two "walks" shows that you have a grouping with two taps, or beats. Count "One-two" as you tap.

DRUMMER 1	1 Walk 2 walk	1 2	1 Walk 2 walk	1 2
DRUMMER 2		1 Walk 2 walk		1 Walk 2 walk

You can substitute two runs in place of a "walk," or you can use a "walk, hold" in place of two "walks." You still feel a two-beat pattern.

DRUMMER 1	1 Walk 2 run run	1 2	1 Walk 2 hold	1 2
DRUMMER 2		1 Walk 2 run run		1 Walk 2 hold

Now tap in patterns of four. Count: "One, two, three, four."

DRUMMER 1	1 Walk 2 walk 3 walk 4 walk	1 2 3 4
DRUMMER 2		1 Walk 2 walk 3 walk 4 walk

Here is a variation.

DRUMMER 1	1 Walk 2 hold 3 run run 4 run run	1 2 3 4
DRUMMER 2		1 Walk 2 hold 3 run run 4 run run

Now tap in patterns of three, and then try your own variations.

DRUMMER 1	1 Walk 2 walk 3 walk	1 2 3
DRUMMER 2		1 Walk 2 walk 3 walk

14

Rhymes and Rhythms

Many rhymes you know fall into regular patterns of two, three, or four beats. Try "Rich Man, Poor Man." It falls into a two-beat pattern. Let Drummer 1 set up the pattern of beats on his drum. Let Drummer 2 tap the rhythm of the rhyme. The pattern of beats and the rhyme fit together as shown below. Notice that "beggar" is two running taps but "thief" and "chief" are both "walk, hold."

	1	2	1	2	1	2	1	2
DRUMMER 1	**Walk**	walk	**Walk**	walk	**Walk**	walk	**Walk**	walk
	Rich	man,	Poor	man,	Beggar	man,	Thief	—,
DRUMMER 2	**Walk**	walk	**Walk**	walk	**Run** run	walk	**Walk**	hold

	1	2	1	2	1	2	1	2
DRUMMER 1	**Walk**	walk	**Walk**	walk	**Walk**	walk	**Walk**	walk
	Doc -	tor,	Law -	yer,	Mer -	chant,	Chief	—.
DRUMMER 2	**Walk**	walk	**Walk**	walk	**Walk**	walk	**Walk**	hold

15

Yankee Doodle

"Yankee Doodle" falls into a pattern of four beats or pulses. Let Drummer 1 set up the pattern. He can count "One-two-three-four" as he taps. Drummer 2 will tap the rhythm of the words as he says them. The rhythm and words fit together like this:

	1	2	3	4	1	2	3	4
DRUMMER 1	Walk	walk	walk	walk	Walk	walk	walk	walk
	Yan-kee	Doo-dle	went to	town, a-	rid-ing	on a	po —	ny. He
DRUMMER 2	Run run	run run	run run	run run	Run run	run run	walk	run run

	1	2	3	4	1	2	3	4
DRUMMER 1	Walk	walk	walk	walk	Walk	walk	walk	walk
	stuck a	fea-ther	in his	cap and	called it	Mac-a-	ro-	ni.
DRUMMER 2	Run run	run run	run run	run run	Run run	run run	walk	walk

You can try this by yourself, using both hands. Tap the beat pattern with your left hand while you tap the rhythm of "Yankee Doodle" with the right hand.

16

Different Beat Patterns

Here is a song for a windy summer night that fits a pattern of three beats. Drummer 1 sets up a pattern of three beats and counts "One-two-three." Drummer 2 taps the rhythm of the rhyme.

	1	2	3	1	2	3
DRUMMER 1	**Walk**	walk	walk	**Walk**	walk	walk
DRUMMER 2	Wild	star-ry	night	Me-te-	ors in	flight
	Walk	run run	walk	**Run** run	run run	walk

	1	2	3	1	2	3
DRUMMER 1	**Walk**	walk	walk	**Walk**	walk	walk
DRUMMER 2	Pin-	points of	light	Like a	dia-mond	bright.
	Walk	run run	walk	**Run** run	run run	walk

Rhythms from India often have irregular beat patterns. Here is a 7-beat pattern. Drummer 2 claps as shown while Drummer 1 taps the beat pattern. Dotted lines show how beats are grouped.

	1	2	3	4	5	6	7	1
DR. 1	**Walk**	walk	**Walk**	walk	**Walk**	**Walk**	**Walk**	**Walk**
2	**Clap**	—	**Clap**	—	**Clap**	**Clap**	—	**Clap**

Repeat

Here is a pattern with eleven beats.

	1	2	3	4	5	6	7	8
DR. 1	**Walk**	walk	walk	walk	**Walk**	walk	walk	walk
2	**Clap**	—	—	—	**Clap**	—	—	—

	9	10	11	1
DR. 1	**Walk**	**Walk**	walk	**Walk**
2	**Clap**	**Clap**	—	**Clap**

Repeat

African Drum Rhythms

Sometimes it is fun to mix patterns. African drummers are very good at playing different rhythms together. You can try mixing the beat patterns you know. Have Drummer 1 play a steady beat of two while Drummer 2 taps a beat pattern of three, as shown below. Make sure you are tapping the "walks" at the same speed before you begin. Give a heavy tap on the first beat of each pattern, as indicated by the underlined words.

| DRUMMER 1 | <u>Walk</u> walk | <u>Walk</u> walk | <u>Walk</u> walk | <u>Walk</u> Hold |
| DRUMMER 2 | <u>Walk</u> walk walk | <u>Walk</u> walk walk | <u>Walk</u> Hold |

Repeat

You can vary the pattern by having Drummer 1 substitute two running taps for the second "walk," as shown below.

| DRUMMER 1 | <u>Walk</u> run run | <u>Walk</u> run run | <u>Walk</u> run run | <u>Walk</u> Hold |
| DRUMMER 2 | <u>Walk</u> walk walk | <u>Walk</u> walk walk | <u>Walk</u> Hold |

Repeat

Here is a variation that Drummer 2 can try.

| DRUMMER 1 | <u>Walk</u> walk | <u>Walk</u> walk | <u>Walk</u> walk | <u>Walk</u> Hold |
| DRUMMER 2 | <u>Walk</u> run run run run | <u>Walk</u> run run run run | <u>Walk</u> Hold |

Repeat

Here is the rhythm of an African children's song. The first player will tap the rhythm on his drum. The second player will clap. You will discover that the clapping creates an interesting pattern against the drummer's rhythm. Clap on each walk and on the second run.

	1	2	3	4	1	2
DRUMMER	<u>W a l k</u>	w a l k	w a l k	w a l k	<u>Run</u> run	run run
CLAPPER	<u>C l a p</u>	c l a p	c l a p	c l a p	— clap	— —

DRUMMER	<u>W a l k</u>	w a l k	w a l k	w a l k	<u>Run</u> run	run run
CLAPPER	<u>C l a p</u>	c l a p	c l a p	c l a p	— clap	— —

Invent rhythmic patterns of your own that sound interesting when played together.

Picturing Rhythms

Suppose you want to remember the rhythms you try on your drums. You can invent ways of picturing rhythms. Many years ago the Egyptians invented a symbol to express the idea "to go." It looked like this:

The symbol for a walking tap in music looks much like the Egyptian symbol. Two taps are written like this:

Below is a chart that shows you how other rhythms are pictured in this book.

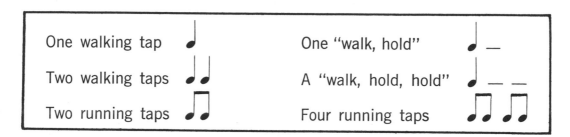

One walking tap		One "walk, hold"	
Two walking taps		A "walk, hold, hold"	
Two running taps		Four running taps	

Here is a rhyme and a picture of its rhythm.

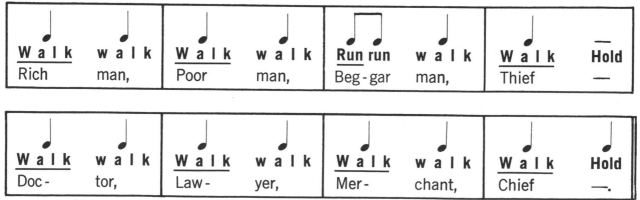

| **W a l k** | w a l k | **W a l k** | w a l k | **Run run** | w a l k | **W a l k** | **Hold** |
| Rich | man, | Poor | man, | Beg - gar | man, | Thief | — |

| **W a l k** | w a l k | **W a l k** | w a l k | **W a l k** | w a l k | **W a l k** | **Hold** |
| Doc - | tor, | Law - | yer, | Mer - | chant, | Chief | —. |

Rhythms for Two Songs

Here are the words of an old song to tap on your drums. The repeated lines give an echo effect if you tap softly for all — except of course "Fire, fire!" The song follows a two-beat pattern.

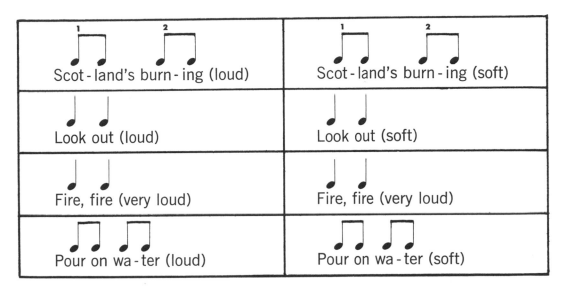

Find a sheet of paper and on it picture the rhythm of a song or rhyme you know. You might try "Are You Sleeping?" First tap the rhythm on your drum as you say the words. It begins with four even walking taps.

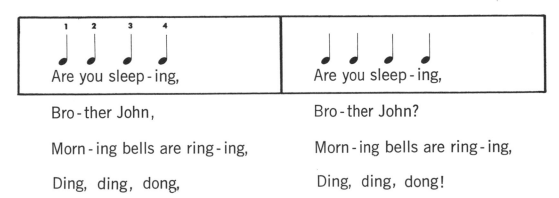

Bro-ther John,   Bro-ther John?

Morn-ing bells are ring-ing,   Morn-ing bells are ring-ing,

Ding, ding, dong,   Ding, ding, dong!

If each line is equal to four walking taps, you have probably marked it correctly. You can check by turning to page 29.

Other Rhythm Instruments

Claves

Maracas

Claves (pronounced klah'vase) are simple to make. Anything you can hold easily in your hand can be used for claves. Those used in a symphony orchestra are made from hardwood. One of the pair of claves is cupped in the hand and the other is tapped against it.

You can make your claves from a broom handle, bamboo, or a thick dowel rod. You will need a saw.

Bamboo is cut with a hacksaw. Your claves will last longer if you cut two sections with nodes at each end. Cup one section in the left hand and tap with the other piece of bamboo. Try out your different rhythms.

Any little box filled with rice or dried beans will make a maraca. You can also use a section of bamboo. Drill a hole in one end, fill the section with grain, then plug the hole.

If you want maracas with handles, like those from Mexico, find two plastic containers with lids. Punch a hole through the center of the lid and bottom of each container. Put rice, dried beans, or corn in the container. If the plastic is transparent, you can color the rice or beans with food dye.

Push the wooden dowel rod through the holes in the lid and bottom of the container. Wrap tape around the rod to hold the handle in place.

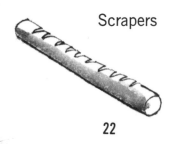

Scrapers

Another Mexican rhythm instrument is a scraper. File notches across a piece of bamboo or broomstick. Scrape across the notches with a stick to make a rhythmic sound.

Making Other Rhythm Instruments

Gongs can be made from many things: odd pieces of metal pipe, red clay flowerpots, pot lids (stainless steel is excellent), bamboo, old railroad spikes, and just plain pieces of wood.

To make a good sound, your gong must be hung so that it will ring when you strike it with a mallet. Here are ways to do this.

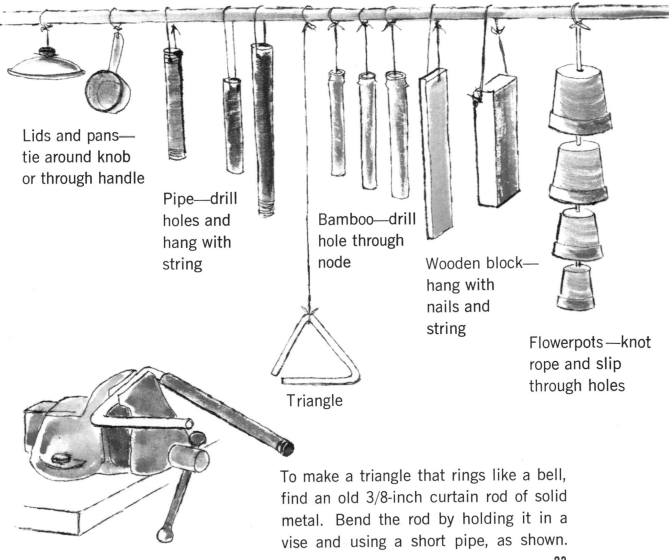

Lids and pans—
tie around knob
or through handle

Pipe—drill
holes and
hang with
string

Bamboo—drill
hole through
node

Wooden block—
hang with
nails and
string

Flowerpots—knot
rope and slip
through holes

Triangle

To make a triangle that rings like a bell, find an old 3/8-inch curtain rod of solid metal. Bend the rod by holding it in a vise and using a short pipe, as shown.

23

More Rhythm Instruments to Make

Tambourines

Make a hoop of 1/8- or 1/4-inch plywood from a piece about 2 inches wide and 24 or more inches long. Soak the plywood overnight before you try to bend it. An easy way to do this is to wrap the wood in a damp cloth and then in plastic to keep the moisture in.

Cover the hoop in the same way you covered the drum (pages 10-11) and paint a design on it.

Collect old pop bottle caps. Remove the cork lining and punch a hole with a nail in the center of each top.

Punch or drill holes in the wood of the tambourine and attach the bottle tops with thin wire.

Bones

Hold firmly

Hold loosely

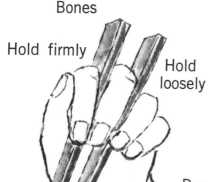

You can get a very unusual sound from bones —which can, but don't have to, be real bones. They are seldom played today because so few people know how to play them. All you need are two sticks 8 inches long, 1 inch wide, 1/8 inch thick. Two dried out beef ribs 8 inches long can be used. Bones are not easy to learn, but try anyway.

Don't move the hand.
Rotate the wrist back and forth rhythmically and the bones will sound.

24

Using Your New Instruments

Tap questions with your claves. Let your friend tap answers on his tambourine.

"What is your name?" "My name is Henry Jonathan
Edward Smith." (Use your own name)

"Where do you live?" "I live at 5 Emerald Street on
the moon ." (Use your own address)

"What is the sum of 10 "The answer is . . . ."
plus 100 plus 1000?"

Find the names of states that have the same rhythm as:

I-o-wa   O-hi-o   Mas-sa-chu-setts   New York

Tap the rhythm on your tambourine.

With Drum and Gong

Use your drum to tap out your own rhythms. Have a friend echo your rhythms on his gong. Keep the patterns short and take turns at beginning and copying. Here are some patterns you might like to try.

A line under a ♩ means a heavier beat or accent.
This — means "hold" for one walking tap.

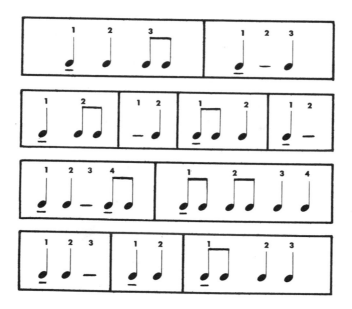

To keep your rhythm moving, you can substitute a light tap on the side of your drum in place of a hold. Sometimes it is fun to tap out the rhythm of words or nonsense syllables such as "Yakkity, yakkity, yak" or "Nickity, nackity, nack" or

Fee, fie, foe, fum,
Tiddledy, taddledy,
Tum, tum, tum.

Make a rhythm out of words for bell sounds—
Ding dong, ding dong,
Ting-a-ling-a, ting-a-ling-a,
Bong —, bong —,
Bong.

Playing in a Rhythm Group

Find friends to play your rhythm instruments and form a rhythm group. Here is a piece you might like to try. Each player has his own rhythmic pattern to follow. Each pattern equals three beats.

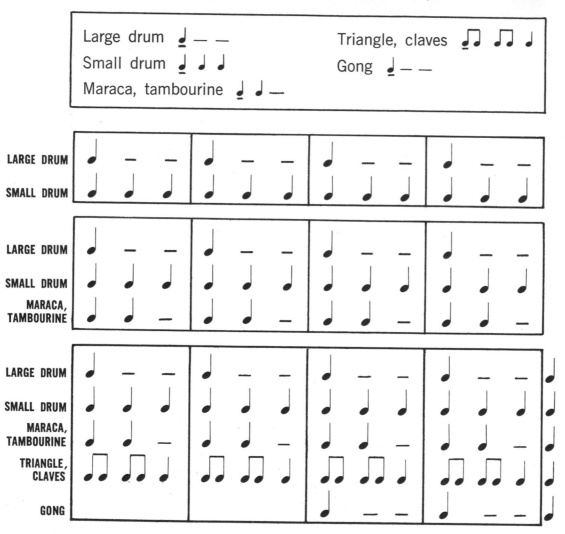

Drummers play their pattern four times, then maraca and tambourine players come in while drummers continue. Triangle and claves players follow, and the gong comes last. With the third tap on the gong, the piece is over. Choose a leader to keep you together.

Are You Sleeping?

You have probably sung "Are You Sleeping?" as a round. Divide your rhythm players into two groups and try the song as a rhythmic round. You can sing right along with your tapping. The groups will fit together as shown below. Group 1 begins, and Group 2 enters on the word "Brother."

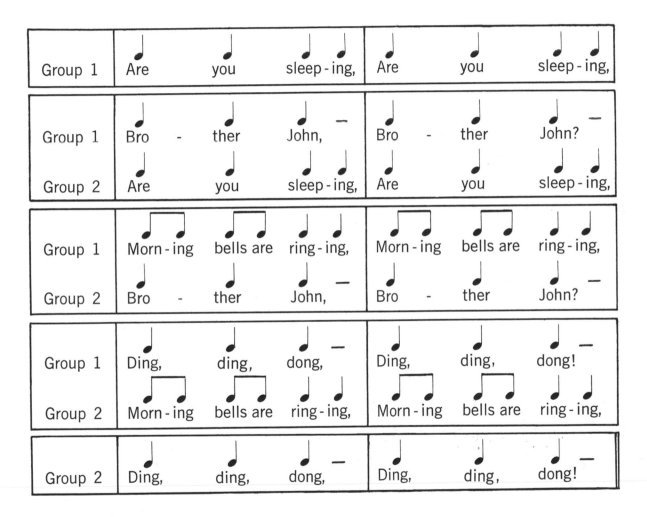

You might think of saving the tambourine and bells for the third line, "Morning bells are ringing." If you have a gong, you might use it on "Ding, ding, dong."

29

Scotland's Burning

"Scotland's Burning" can also be used as a round. Say the words as you tap the rhythm patterns.

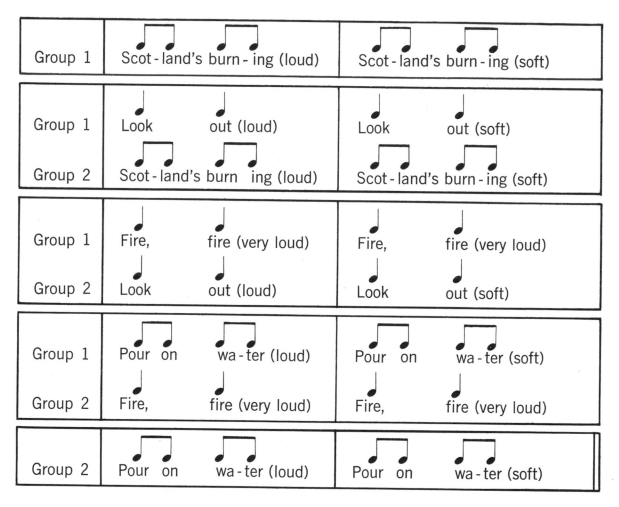

Group 1	Scot-land's burn-ing (loud)	Scot-land's burn-ing (soft)
Group 1	Look out (loud)	Look out (soft)
Group 2	Scot-land's burn ing (loud)	Scot-land's burn-ing (soft)
Group 1	Fire, fire (very loud)	Fire, fire (very loud)
Group 2	Look out (loud)	Look out (soft)
Group 1	Pour on wa-ter (loud)	Pour on wa-ter (soft)
Group 2	Fire, fire (very loud)	Fire, fire (very loud)
Group 2	Pour on wa-ter (loud)	Pour on wa-ter (soft)

You can also sing a song that you know and use your rhythm instruments to accompany your singing. Play along with dance music on the radio, TV, or your favorite records.

30

A One-Man Band

You can be a one-man band with all of your rhythm instruments. Tap from one instrument to the next in different rhythmic patterns. Listen to the different sounds of your instruments.

The next time you hear a band or an orchestra play, listen especially to the sounds of the percussion instruments. Listen to the rhythms the percussion player creates with his instruments.

Playing Your Rhythm Instruments

Here is a picture guide for a piece which uses your percussion instruments. Line up your instruments as pictured. The piece uses your instruments from left to right and back again.

It follows a four-beat pattern.

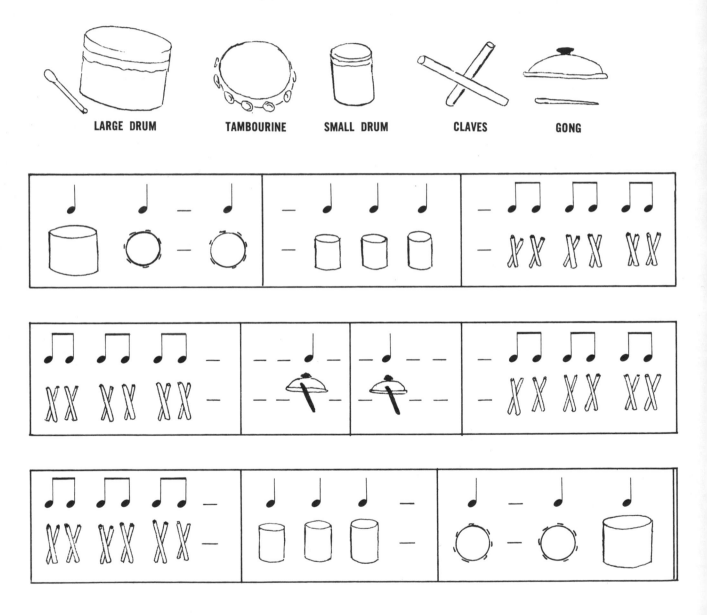

LARGE DRUM   TAMBOURINE   SMALL DRUM   CLAVES   GONG

Discovering Sounds

You have discovered the many different sounds your rhythm instruments make. Now tap on different things around your house, inside and out, and see what interesting sounds you can discover.

Sounds have different qualities.
>   Run a stick along a picket fence.
>   Tap on something deep and hollow.
>   Tap on wood, tap on glass, tap on steel.
>   Listen to the sounds of words like murmur, buzz, squawk.

Sounds are high and low.
>   Listen to the sounds of voices. Some voices sound high, and others sound very low. Who of your friends or family has a high voice? Who has a low voice? Listen to singers and notice whether their voices sound high or low.

Sounds have pitch.
>   When you speak of a definite sound that is sung or played on an instrument, you are talking about its pitch.

Musical pitches are named according to the first seven letters of the alphabet, **A**, **B**, **C**, **D**, **E**, **F**, **G**.

The same group of pitches can be sung very high or very, very low. The same group of pitches can be raised, that is made sharp, or lowered, that is made flat.

Experiments with Voice Sounds

Make high sounds and low sounds and in-between sounds with your voice. Make loud sounds, soft sounds, short sounds, long drawn-out sounds. Sing up with your voice, and then sing down again.

Listen to the way a melody goes up and down in a song you know.

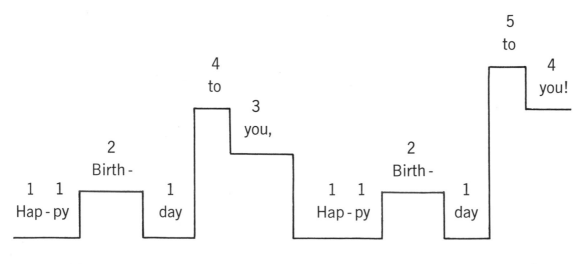

Inventing Your Own Melodies

Try making a melody with your singing voice. Take a word, "Hallelujah" (sung hal-e-loo´-ya). First sing Hallelujah in a steady walking rhythm on one tone or pitch.

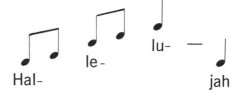

Hal - le - lu - jah

Now sing up with your voice as you move to the third syllable, then drop back to where you began as you sing the last syllable.

Hal- le- lu- jah

Sing the same pattern in a very high singing voice and in a low voice.

Now sing the same pattern, but change the rhythm. On the third syllable, hold the sound before dropping to the last syllable.

Hal- le- lu- — jah

Here is another pattern to sing.

Hal- le- lu- jah

Try your own patterns of melody and rhythm for "Hallelujah." Look for other words and expressions to use. You might try creating a melody to your favorite poem or rhyme.

Man and His Instruments

Men have not only used their voices to make sounds but have fashioned instruments to make music. They have invented percussion instruments to play rhythms. They have learned to get a variety of sounds from plucking or bowing strings. They have also invented many kinds of blowing instruments.

The best way to find out about instruments is to make your own and experiment with them for yourself. Listen at the same time to many kinds of music on radio, television, at the movies, and on your own record player. Listen to as much live music as you can to become aware of different sounds and how they are produced.

How a Bugle Is Blown

Our first experiments will show us how brass players, buglers, and trumpet players make their sounds.

Find a piece of pipe about one foot long with an inside diameter of ½ inch. Wrap tape around one end to form a mouth-piece.

To amplify the sound, cut the bottom off a gallon or half-gallon plastic bottle. Put enough tape around the pipe so that it fits snugly into the mouth of the bottle.

Drill finger holes as illustrated. Press your lips firmly against the mouthpiece and blow. The trick is to vibrate your lips a little to produce a sound. Use the holes, covering and uncovering them with your fingers, to vary the sound.

The next time you see and hear an orchestra or band play, be sure to watch the brass players and listen carefully to the sounds of their instruments.

How Reed Instruments Are Blown

Reeds vibrate to make sound. Some blowing instruments use a reed to help make their sound. Clarinet and saxophone players use a single reed. Oboe and bassoon players use a double reed. Even a bagpipe player uses a double reed.

Reeds are made of bamboo, but in our experiment we will use an ordinary plastic straw.

Slit the straw about one inch. Punch or burn two or three holes in the other end of the straw. Hold the slit end in warm water for a few minutes, then press the ends together with your thumb and finger. Place the flattened end in your mouth and blow. You should feel it tickle your lips a little as it vibrates to make a sound. The tone can be changed by making the slit longer or cutting off the straw.

Look in your record shop for records of reed players from all over the world.

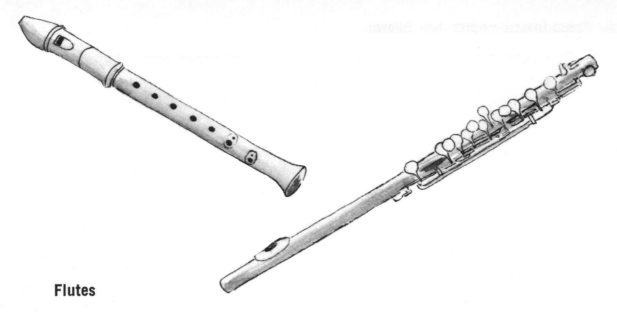

Flutes

There are different kinds of flutes. One kind is held in front and blown like a whistle. The recorder is an instrument like this. There is another kind of flute that is held to the side. The sound is produced by blowing across a hole in the mouthpiece and this sets air in motion in the flute. You will see this kind of flute in an orchestra.

You can make a sound like this flute produces by blowing across a bottle. Try different sized bottles for high and low sounds. You will have a flute orchestra.

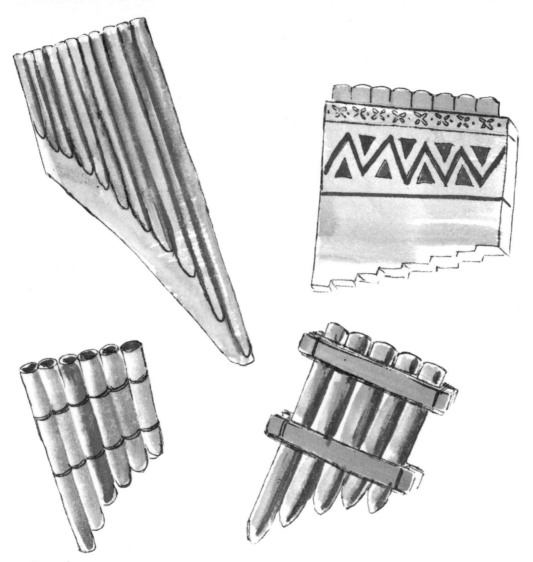

Panpipes

In the ancient world, we find another flutelike instrument, the pan-pipes. Panpipes are made up of a number of tubes of different length fastened together. This simple instrument is named for Pan, the Greek god of forests and pastures. The sound of the panpipes is made by blowing across the openings at the top of the pipe. You can make panpipes from rubber shower hose and learn to play melodies on them.

A Set of Panpipes to Make

The panpipes you will make are measured to give the pitches **G, A, B, D, E,** which make the pentatonic scale. This five-tone scale has been used for hundreds of years all over the world. You can make and play many melodies using this scale.

What You Will Need: Two feet of rubber shower hose, 3/8 inch in diameter, from hardware store; dowel rod, 3/8 inch size; glue; ruler, scissors, pencil, saw, cardboard.

What to Do

Tie a small weight to one end of hose and let it hang overnight to straighten out.

For a 5-pipe instrument, measure shower hose to these lengths:

1st pipe: 4½ inches	3rd pipe: 3¾ inches
2nd pipe: 4 inches	4th pipe: 3½ inches
	5th pipe: 3¼ inches

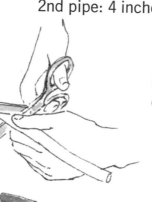

Pinch the end of the hose as you cut to get a straight edge.

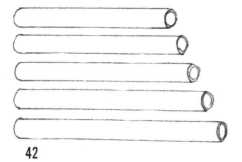

Cut the dowel rod into five pieces, each about an inch long.

The measurements given for the inside length of the pipes are to the nearest sixteenth of an inch so that you will have a well-tuned instrument.

Insert a dowel rod into the first pipe. Mark your pencil at 3-15/16 inches, as illustrated. This will be the length of the inside for the first pipe. Insert the pencil into the 4-1/2 inch pipe until it reaches the mark on your pencil. This will be the correct inside length for this pipe. Mark it **G.**

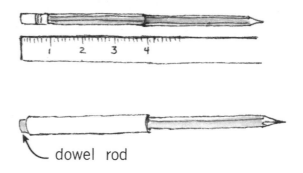

dowel rod

Here are pitches and measurements for the other four pipes.

A (2nd pipe) Mark pencil at 3–7/16″, insert in 4″ hose.

B (3rd pipe) Mark pencil at 3–1/16″, insert in 3–3/4″ hose.

D (4th pipe) Mark pencil at 2–1/2″, insert in 3–1/2″ hose.

E (5th pipe) Mark pencil at 2–3/16″, insert in 3–1/4″ hose.

Be sure to mark each pipe with the letter name for its pitch.

Cut two pieces of stiff cardboard 2 inches wide and about 4 inches long. Glue the pipes to one cardboard piece, as shown, leaving about 1/2 inch between pipes.

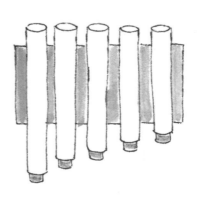

Glue the other cardboard over the top and place a book on the pipes. Your panpipes should be ready to play in an hour. You can paint designs on the cardboard as a final touch.

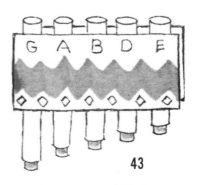

43

Playing Your Panpipes

Now you are ready to try your panpipes. If you have carefully measured the inside lengths of your pipes, you have an instrument that plays the pentatonic scale: **G, A, B, D, E**.

Hold the panpipes so that the low tone, **G**, is on the left and the high tone, **E**, is on the right.

Hold the open end of the pipe you are blowing firmly against the top of the lip, as shown. Tighten the lip as you blow across the pipe opening.

Say "to-o" as you blow, and aim the stream of air toward the opposite inside edge of the pipe. You may need to tilt the bottom of the pipes away from you to get the right angle for hitting the inside edge. Keep the stream of air flowing to support your tone.

To see if you are blowing correctly, hold one hand in front of the pipes. Blow across the opening. If half of the air you are blowing hits your hand and the other half hits the inside of the pipe, you are blowing correctly and should get a good sound. Sing the sound of each pipe after you blow it.

Melodies for Panpipes

Begin on the lowest-sounding pipe and blow up the pentatonic scale, **G**, **A**, **B**, **D**, **E**. Then sing the scale.

Next, begin with the highest-sounding pipe and blow down the pentatonic scale. **E**, **D**, **B**, **A**, **G**. Sing down the scale.

Imagine you are a flute player.
Blow your own tunes. Begin with
your name. It might go like this.

D	**B**	**E**	**D**	**E**
John — ny		Ap — ple — seed		

Blow a tune to "Rich Man, Poor Man."
Have a friend help you keep in rhythm
by tapping the rhyme on his drums.

Here is one way to play "Rich Man, Poor Man."
Play the pipes as marked above each word.

D B	**D B**	**D D E**	**D —**
Rich man,	Poor man,	Beg - gar man,	Thief, —
D B	**D B**	**A A**	**B —**
Doc - tor,	Law - yer,	Mer - chant,	Chief. —

Open up a book of rhymes or poems and play melodies to the rhythm of the ones you like best.

Goodbye, Old Paint

Here is on old cowboy song to try on your panpipes. The words fall into a three-beat pattern. Have a drummer tap the three-beat pattern slowly. Clap and speak the words in rhythm, as shown. On "bye" and "Paint," shake your hand to the side to mark the one-beat hold. When you know the rhythm, pick up your panpipes and blow. The letters above each word tell you what pipes to play. Notice that the melody begins on the drummer's third beat.

Part 1.

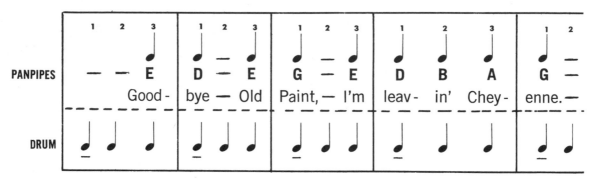

When you blow the first part of the song, then move on to the second part, shown below. After the second part, repeat Part 1.

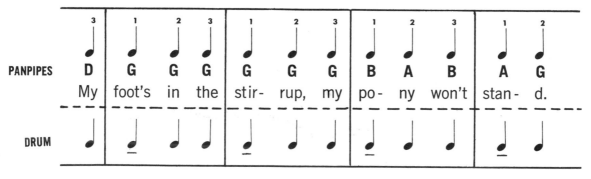

(Repeat Part I)

46

Invent many melodies of your own on the panpipes. Play to the rhythm of a drummer or have a drummer make a rhythm to your music.

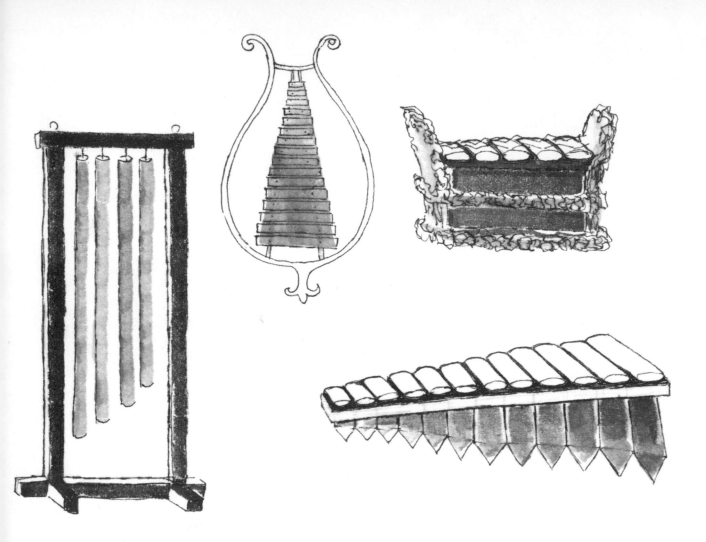

Percussion Instruments

All over the world you will find instruments that produce a sound when struck with a mallet or the hand. Instruments that are struck are called percussion instruments. All of the rhythm instruments, such as drums, gongs, and tambourines, are percussion instruments.

Some percussion instruments can make melodies. Here are pictures of several of them. Even a piano is considered a percussion instrument. The sound of the piano is produced by hammers striking on the strings.

Making a Metallophone

Any striking instrument made from metal is called a metallophone. You can make a pentatonic metallophone by cutting different kinds of pipe to size for certain pitches. You can buy electric thin-wall conduit pipe or aluminum tubing in a hardware store to make your instrument.

Thin-wall conduit comes in sizes, 3/4 inch diameter and 1/2 inch diameter. Aluminum tubing can be bought polished or unpolished in two sizes, 3/4 inch outside diameter or 1 inch. Both come in 6-foot lengths. The aluminum tubing is sometimes called "do-it-yourself" aluminum. It is softer and easier to saw than the steel, and just a little more expensive.

You can cut both kinds of metal tubing with a hacksaw. Use a blade with 18 teeth to the inch for steel, and a blade with 24 teeth to the inch for aluminum.

The chart below shows you the measurements for each pitch for each kind of pipe. You will have a low-sounding pentatonic scale which you can mark G_I, A_I, B_I, D_I, E_I for your first range.

	ELECTRIC THIN-WALL CONDUIT		UNPOLISHED ALUMINUM	POLISHED ALUMINUM	
	1/2"	3/4"	1"	1"	3/4"
G_I	14–1/2	16–5/8	17–3/16	17–1/2	15–1/8
A_I	13–11/16	15–3/4	16–1/4	16–9/16	14–1/4
B_I	12–15/16	14–13/16	15–5/16	15–5/8	13–7/16
D_I	11–3/4	13–7/16	13–15/16	14–3/16	12–3/16
E_I	11–1/16	12–11/16	13–1/16	13–5/16	11–1/2

In most hardware stores, solid steel curtain rods in a 3/8 inch diameter are cut to order. (These are often called "brass" because they are brass-colored.) Pieces too short to sell are thrown away. You can cut these to size for a very high-pitched metallophone. Maybe the hardware man will cut the rods for you with his machine.

Adjustments in tuning can be made by sawing off a pipe to raise the pitch or using a longer piece of pipe to get a lower pitch.

STEEL CURTAIN RODS				
G_I	A_I	B_I	D_I	E_I
8–15/16	8–3/8	7–15/16	7–1/4	6–13/16

How to Saw Pipe

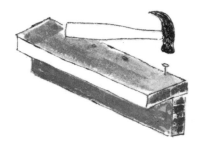

Use a vise to help you hold the pipe in place as you saw. If you don't have a vise, find two pieces of wood about 1x2x12 inches. Nail them together to look like this.

Clamp to the edge of a table or bench.

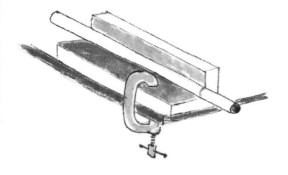

Mark the pipe to the exact sixteenth of an inch for the length you want. Place the pipe in the wooden trough with the mark for cutting at the edge.

Use one hand to hold the pipe firmly against the trough, as illustrated. Hold the hacksaw firmly in the other hand and place the blade flat against the wood. The pipe is easy to cut as long as you let the saw do the work. Use long, easy strokes. Hold the saw firmly, but at the same time keep your arm muscles loose. When you have finished sawing, file the edge to make it smooth.

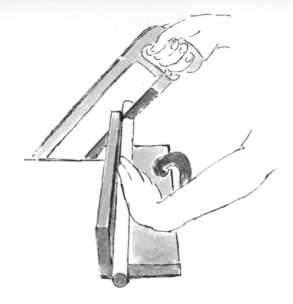

Mark the pipes with tape and pen, G_I, A_I, B_I, D_I, E_I. Place them on two strips of sponge rubber or rolled towels.

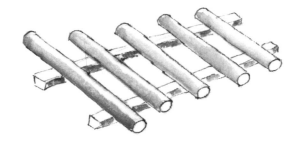

The metallophone can be played with a pencil or a stick. A mallet can be made from 1/4- or 3/8-inch dowel rod, cut to about a 10-inch length. Glue a block of wood at one end, as shown. For a soft mallet, use a cap eraser on the end of a pencil.

Now you are ready to play. Try "Goodbye, Old Paint." Invent your own melodies or invent an accompaniment on your metallophone to go with a song you know.

Oh, Susanna!

All the verses, but not the chorus, of "Oh, Susanna!" can be played on your pipes. Where you see the small "**a**" and "**g**" tap the pipe lightly to mark the hold. A drummer can tap a steady running rhythm to help you play in rhythm. Sing the chorus and accompany yourself with a rhythm instrument. The melody of the chorus uses tones that are not a part of your pentatonic scale.

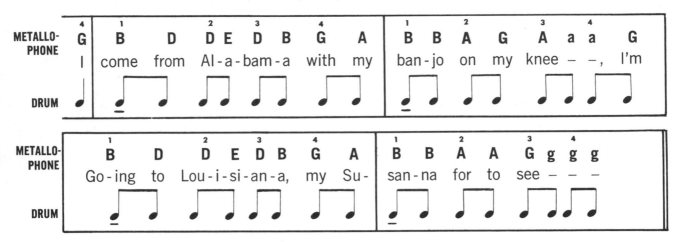

Chorus: Oh, Susanna! Oh, don't you cry for me, I come from Alabama with my banjo on my knee.

Goodbye, Old Paint

You can play an accompaniment figure on your metallophone to a melody on your panpipes. Here is a pattern for the metallophone player to learn for "Goodbye, Old Paint."

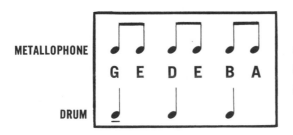

A repeated pattern like this is called an ostinato (pronounced ahs te nad'o).

Practice the pattern with a drummer, who will play a steady 3-beat pattern. Next, have the panpipes player practice his melody with the drummer. Now put the parts together. The metallophone player begins his pattern on the first beat, and the panpipes player begins on the third beat. Have the drummer count "1—2—3" as you play to help keep everyone together. Play slowly. When you have learned the song, ask other friends to play on their rhythm instruments. Let them imitate a horse's trot.

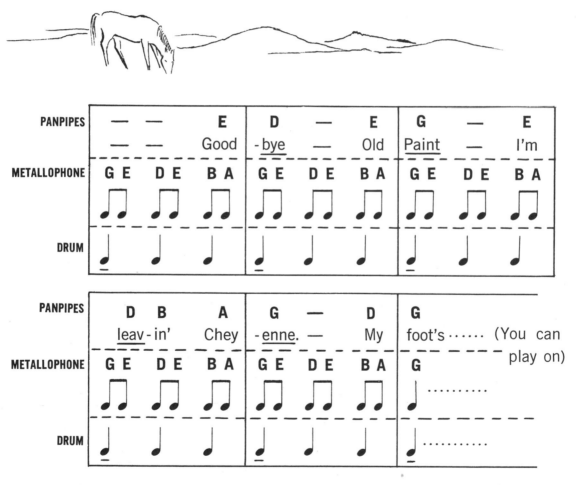

Take turns using the different instruments.

Another Metallophone

You can make a second set of pipes that will give you the penta-tonic scale in a higher voice. With a double set of pipes you will be able to play more melodies. Here are the measurements to follow. When you have finished, mark the pipes G_2, A_2, B_2, D_2, E_2.

	ELECTRIC THIN-WALL CONDUIT		UNPOLISHED ALUMINUM	POLISHED ALUMINUM		STEEL CURTAIN RODS
	1/2″	3/4″	1″	3/4″	1″	3/8″
G_2	10–1/16″	11–1/2″	11-15/16″	10-7/16″	12-3/16″	6-1/4″
A_2	9–1/2	10-13/16	11-3/16	9-13/16	11-3/8	5-15/16
B_2	8–15/16	10-3/16	10-1/2	9-1/4	10-3/4	5-9/16
D_2	8–1/8	9-1/4	9-9/16	8-7/16	9-3/4	5-1/16
E_2	7–11/16	8-3/4	9-1/16	8	9-3/16	4-13/16

A Pocket Glockenspiel

You can tie your pipes together with string, as illustrated. After the knots are tightened, add a little white glue to each knot to hold the pipes in place. You can carry this metallophone around in your hip pocket and use it for a marching band or an impromptu clambake. Call it your pocket glockenspiel and impress your friends.

You can tie both the steel and the aluminum pipes in this way, as well as curtain rods.

Playing Your Metallophones

Here is a very old pentatonic tune that will be easy to play on your double set of pipes. It is the tune of an old nursery rhyme—see if you can tell what it is. You will need practice to play the pipes in a running rhythm. You can begin by practicing slowly.

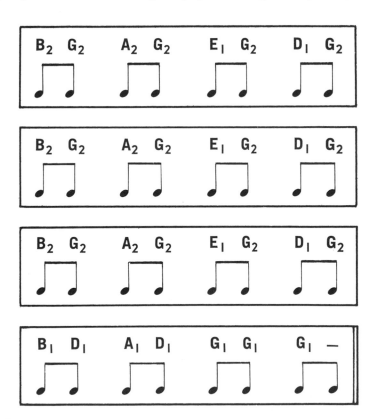

Making a Xylophone

It will be fun for you to make a xylophone if you have a partner to help you—someone to hold the wood while you saw, someone to discover the right pitch with you, and of course someone to help you clean up when you are finished.

This chart shows approximate sizes for a xylophone tuned to a low pentatonic scale (G_1, A_1, B_1, D_1, E_1) and a high one (G_2, A_2, B_2, D_2, E_2) made from screen stock or redwood. Screen stock in a 1x2 size is available in hardware stores and lumberyards. Redwood pickets in 1x3 or 1x4 sizes can be found in lumberyards; this wood gives a full, ringing sound.

	1x2 SCREEN STOCK	1x3 REDWOOD	1x4 REDWOOD		1x2 SCREEN STOCK	1x3 REDWOOD	1x4 REDWOOD
G_1	19″	19–1/2″	18–1/2″	G_2	13″	13–1/2″	13–1/4″
A_1	18	19	17–3/4	A_2	12–1/2	12–1/4	12–1/4
B_1	17–1/2	18	17–1/4	B_2	12	11–1/2	12
D_1	16	16	16–1/2	D_2	11	10	11
E_1	15	14	16	E_2	10	9–1/4	10–1/4

Tune to **G**, **A**, **B** below middle **C**
D, **E** above middle **C**

Tune to **G** above middle **C**
followed by **A**, **B**, **D**, **E**

Buy the amount of wood you will need, allowing something extra for recutting bars if necessary. If you are using 1x2 screen stock, for example, you might buy ten feet. You will also need a cardboard box 18x15x10 inches; glue; two narrow strips of wood, rope, felt, or foam rubber; pencil and ruler.

You will use a hacksaw and miter box for the sawing. If you don't have these around the house, any saw will do. You can use a clamp or ask your friend to hold the wood as you saw. Most of all, you will need patience.

To get the best sound from a bar, rest it on a piece of rope or felt at its two nodal points. Here is how to establish those points. They are a little more than one fourth of the distance from each end.

Mark the nodal points and place the bar on a piece of rope at each point. Hit the bar in the center for a good tone, using your metallophone mallet or a pencil.

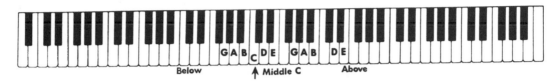

Tuning means to match the pitch of a bar to a definite standard pitch. You can tune your xylophone to a high pentatonic scale (G_2, A_2, B_2, D_2, E_2) by using your metallophone marked G_1, A_1, B_1, D_1, E_1. For the low pentatonic scale on the xylophone, tune to a piano. The picture of the piano shows you where to find these pitches.

If the sound of the bar is lower than the sound you are trying to match, saw off the end, a little at a time. You may have to do this five or six times before you get the right pitch. If the bar is higher than it should be, start over with a longer bar. Be sure to buy extra wood for this purpose.

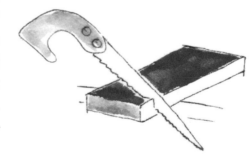

Mount the wood bars on rope or strips of felt or sponge rubber. Use small brads nailed through the rope at the nodal points. Glue two small sticks to the bottom of the ropes. Glue the sticks to the box, as illustrated. The glue should dry in about an hour and then your instrument will be ready to play.

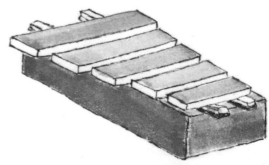

57

Melodies from India for Xylophone or Metallophone

This Indian melody follows the seven-beat pattern you have tried before on your drums. Let the drummer set up the rhythmic pattern of the melody first. The drummer can tap on the side of his drum for the "hold." He should count from one to seven as he taps. After the drummer has played the pattern twice, you can begin the melody. Shake your hand to the side for each hold.

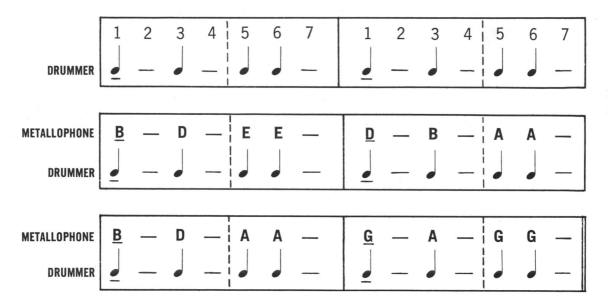

Here is another melody from India. It follows an interesting eleven-beat pattern.

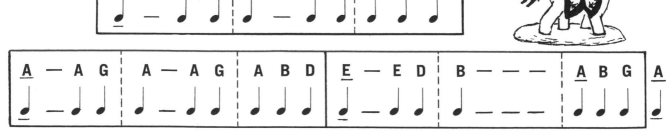

58

Sleep, Baby, Sleep

This is a quiet melody for metallophone or panpipes accompanied by the xylophone.

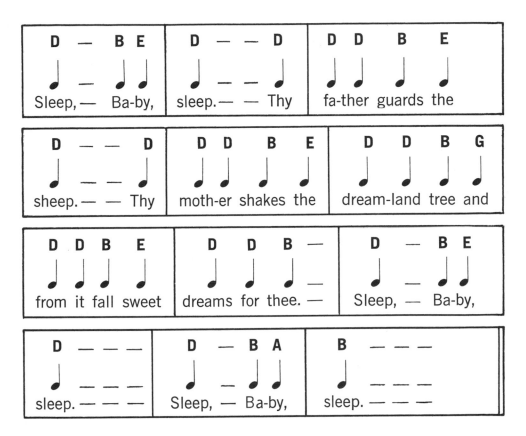

While you play the melody on the pipes, ask a friend to play along with you on the xylophone. Here is a pattern for him to play: **G E D B** in a steady walking rhythm. Have your friend use a padded mallet so that the accompaniment is soft.

It is helpful to begin with a drummer whose job it will be to keep the steady four-beat pattern of the song. The xylophone player will join the drummer. The player on the pipes or the metallophone comes in last. Wait for the drummer's beat on each "hold."

Other rhythm players can join in with a quiet rocking rhythm.

A Riddle Song

This old melody uses the following pipes from your metallophone or xylophone: D_1, E_1, G_2, A_2, B_2, D_2, E_2. Notice how the words fit the 4-beat pattern played by the drummer.

Clap with the words as you speak them and give a shake to the side on each hold. When you know the rhythm, play the pipes as marked. You can play softly on the letters **g, a, b, d, e** to mark the holds.

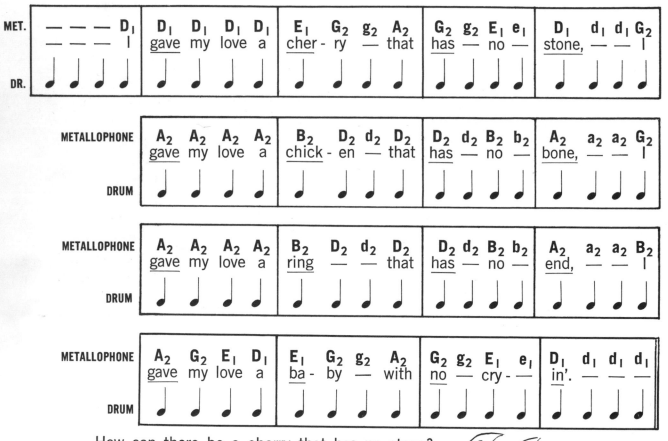

How can there be a cherry that has no stone?
How can there be a chicken that has no bone?
How can there be a ring that has no end?
How can there be a baby with no cryin'?

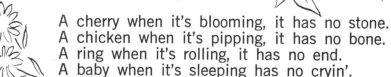

A cherry when it's blooming, it has no stone.
A chicken when it's pipping, it has no bone.
A ring when it's rolling, it has no end.
A baby when it's sleeping has no cryin'.

Inventing Music Together

When you have several instruments, it is fun to invent music together. Have a drummer set up a rhythmic pattern first. The xylophone or metallophone player enters next with a repeated melodic pattern that fits with the rhythm of the drummer. The third player will then play a melody on his instrument.

Here is a pattern to try. All the players' parts fit with the regular 3-beat pattern of the drummer.

You can invent a melody of your own using the rhythmic pattern.

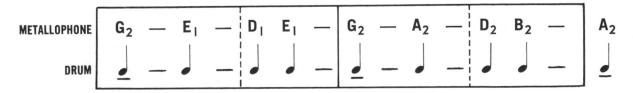

Using your 7-beat pattern from India, try a melody on your metallophone or xylophone using the full set of pipes G_1, A_1, B_1, D_1, E_1, G_2, A_2, B_2, D_2, E_2.

Have a third player clap on the silent beats and another player play the gong on each first beat. Continue your own melody as the drummer plays the rhythm.

61

Making More Music

Using pipes G_1, A_1, B_1, D_1, E_1, G_2, A_2, B_2, D_2, E_2 play two sounds together on your metallophone. Try the pattern below.

RIGHT HAND	B_2	D_2	B_2	A_2
LEFT HAND	G_2	E_1	D_1	E_1

Here is another rhythmic pattern for a friend to use for a melody while you play your pattern on the metallophone.

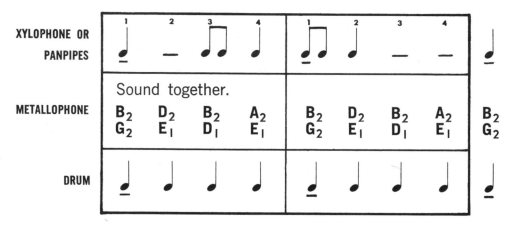

You can change your pattern into a 5-beat pattern, like this:

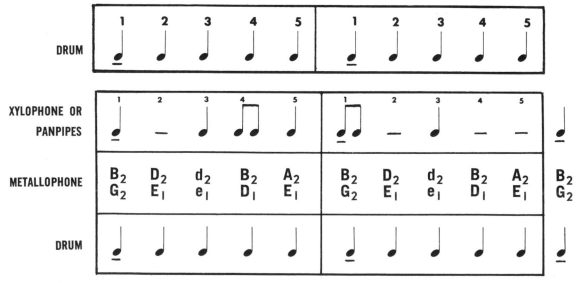

62

John Henry

Try the folk song "John Henry" on your metallophone or xylophone. The drummer should tap the rhythm of the song as you say the words. On each hold, the drummer gives a walking tap on the side of his drum while you give a clap. When you are playing the pipes, have a friend clap and say the words. The song follows a 4-beat pattern.

Use G_1, A_1, B_1, D_1, E_1, G_2, A_2, B_2, D_2, E_2.

A Japanese Pentatonic Scale

In this Japanese scale, a new pipe, B_1 flat (marked $B_1{}^\flat$) takes the place of your B_1 pipe. The scale is G_1, A_1, $B_1{}^\flat$, D_1, E_1.

To flat a note means to lower its sound. The $B_1{}^\flat$ pipe will sound one half step lower than the B_1 pipe. Here are the measurements for a $B_1{}^\flat$ pipe in thin-wall or aluminum.

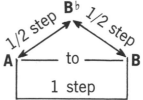

	THIN-WALL	POLISHED ALUMINUM	
	3/4 INCH	3/4 INCH	1 INCH
$B_1{}^\flat$	15–5/16	13–7/8	16–1/8

Try out the sound of your new scale and invent melodies with it.

Expanding the Pentatonic Scale

You can add a pipe to your old pentatonic scale to give you a 6–tone scale. The new pipe C_1 will fall in between B_1 and D_1. Your scale will then be G_1, A_1, B_1, C_1, D_1, E_1.

If you add another pipe to give a D below G_1 you can play "Are You Sleeping?" Your scale will then be D, G_1, A_1, B_1, C_1, D_1, E_1.

	THIN-WALL	POLISHED ALUMINUM	
	3/4 INCH	3/4 INCH	1 INCH
C_1	14–7/16	13–1/16	15–1/8
D	19–3/8	17–1/2	20–3/8

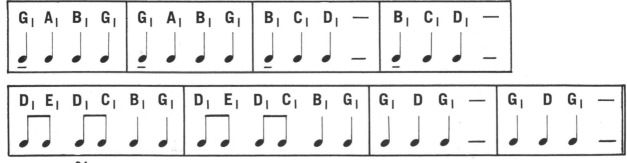

The Major Scale

Many melodies in Western music use the pitches that make up a scale called the major scale. You can make a major scale by adding one new pipe to your 6–tone scale plus the G_2 pipe. Your new pipe will be F_1 sharp (marked $F_1{}^\#$). To sharp a sound means to raise the sound. The $F_1{}^\#$ pipe will sound one half step higher than F_1.

	THIN-WALL	POLISHED ALUMINUM	
	3/4 INCH	3/4 INCH	1 INCH
$F_1{}^\#$	11–13/16	10–3/4	12–3/8

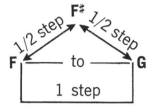

Here is your new scale: G_1, A_1, B_1, C_1, D_1, E_1, $F_1{}^\#$, G_2.

Invent melodies using your major scale. By using the metallophone try to find the melodies for other songs you know.

Try the chorus of "Oh, Susanna!"

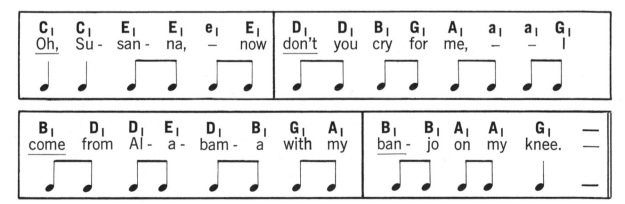

The Minor Scale

Many melodies use the pitches of the minor scale. Make an $E_1{}^\flat$ pipe and then invent melodies using the minor scale, G_1, A_1, $B_1{}^\flat$, C_1, D_1, $E_1{}^\flat$, $F_1{}^\#$, G_2.

	THIN-WALL	POLISHED ALUMINUM	
	3/4 INCH	3/4 INCH	1 INCH
$E_1{}^\flat$	13–1/16	11–7/8	13–3/4

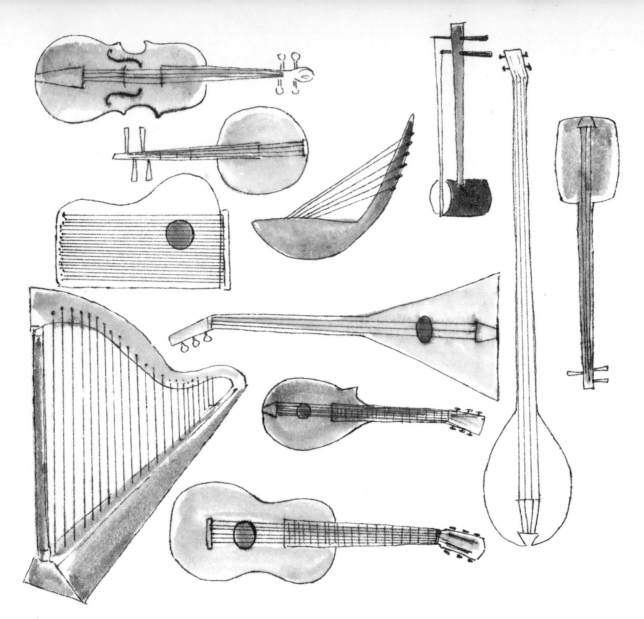

Stringed Instruments

There are many kinds of stringed instruments. There is the double bass that you see in a jazz band, and all the smaller members of that family: the cello, viola, and violin. There are guitars, banjos, lutes, zithers, and harps. There are instruments from other lands, like the koto from Japan, the sitar from India, and the balalaika from Russia. Here are pictures of stringed instruments. Some are plucked, some are bowed, and some, like the dulcimer, are struck.

Strings for Your Instruments

Monofilament nylon fishing line is used for all the stringed instruments in this book except the wooden guitar. You can buy this line wherever fishing supplies are sold. It comes in sizes marked to show the weight the line will hold, for example 6–pound test, 12–pound test, and so on. It is important to use the right size for your instrument to get the desired note or pitch.

If you cannot get the size that is heavy enough, two or three lighter lines can be twisted together. Attach the two or three lighter lines to a nail or knob on your instrument.

Stretch the lines across the instrument and tie them to the eyebolt on the opposite side. Attach the eyebolt to a drill and turn the knob of the drill to twist the line.

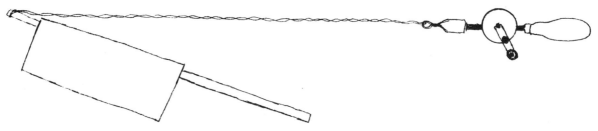

This chart shows line weight to use for different string lengths.

POUND TEST	STRING LENGTH
15	10–19 inches
20	20–24 inches
30	25–30 inches

Note: One 30–pound test line or two 15–pound test lines can be used for 36–inch double bass string for **D**. One 60–pound test or three 20–pound or four 15–pound can be used for 36–inch double bass string for **G**.

Remember, if the string is too loose, it will have a poor sound; if it is too tight, it will easily slip out of tune.

Making a Five-Stringed Box Harp

You can make a box harp with five strings tuned to the pentatonic scale of your metallophone, G_1, A_1, B_1, D_1, E_1.

Materials You Will Need:
1. Cardboard carton with a side measuring 20x10 inches.
2. One piece of wood 12x3/4x1/2 inch. Any piece of wood near this size will do.
3. A second piece of wood, 10x4x1 inch or close to that size.
4. Five eyebolts, 1/4x3 size.
5. Monofilament fishing line, 15–pound test.
6. Friction tape, white glue, masking tape, matchsticks.

Tools: Scroll, hack, or keyhole saw. Drill with 7/32–inch bit.

What to do:
Saw five grooves, 2 inches apart, in the longer piece of wood. Saw about halfway through the wood.

Drill five holes about 2 inches apart in the other piece of wood.

Draw a 45–degree angle on the box, as shown.

Spread glue on the back of the grooved piece of wood. Use masking tape to hold the wood in place along the 45–degree line. Let the glue dry for a few hours and remove the tape.

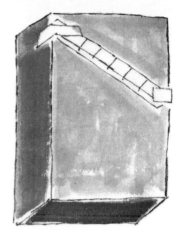

Spread glue on the other piece of wood. Use masking tape to fasten it to the end of the box. Let glue dry, remove tape.

Wrap friction tape around each eyebolt, coming about halfway down. This keeps the monofilament line from slipping as you tune. Screw the eye–bolts into the holes you drilled.

Cut five pieces of monofilament line, each about 6 inches longer than the box.

Tie a piece of wooden matchstick to the end of a piece of line and place it in the groove, as illustrated. Pull the line tight and wrap it two or three times around the taped part of the eyebolt. Tie a knot.

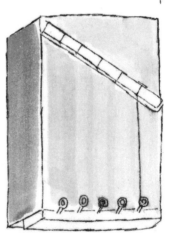

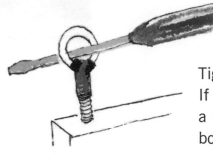

Tighten the line by turning the eyebolt clockwise. If the screw is too difficult to turn by hand, use a screwdriver or large nail through the eye of the bolt for leverage.

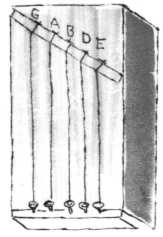

Add the remaining strings in the same way. The longest string will tune to G_1 of your metallophone. The shortest string tunes to E_1. Mark your strings in order, beginning with the longest: **G, A, B, D, E.**

Tuning Your Harp

Before you play your box harp, you need to learn to tune it. The **G, A, B, D, E** strings tune to G_1, A_1, B_1, D_1, E_1 of your metallophone. You can also find these pitches on a piano or on a pitch pipe bought from a music store. Ask for a pitch pipe that gives you pitches going from **F** to **F** above middle **C.**

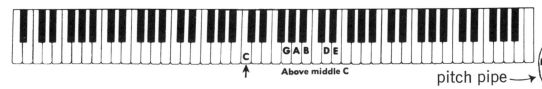

This picture of a piano shows how to find the pentatonic scale you need to tune your box harp. The pitches of the pitch pipe are shown, too.

More About Tuning Your Box Harp

Step by Step

1 Play the **G** of your metallophone, piano, or pitch pipe. Sing the tone that you hear. Be sure the tone you sing is the same tone you hear.

2 Sing this tone as you turn the eyebolt at the end of your box harp. Turn this eyebolt for the longest string clockwise to tighten the string. Pluck the string. When the string sounds the same as your voice, it should be in tune. Be sure to keep plucking the string as you turn the eyebolt.

3 Check the sound of your string on your harp with the **G** on your metallophone, piano, or pitch pipe. If your harp sounds the same, the string is in tune. If you tighten the string too much, you will get a sound higher than **G**. Turn the eyebolt in the opposite direction to lower the sound. It always takes a little time and careful listening to tune. Don't be in a hurry.

4 Repeat the first three steps for the four strings that are left— **A, B, D, E.** Check all five strings when you have tuned them to hear whether they sound like the pentatonic scale. You may need to do some retuning before your harp is all in tune. Always tune your instrument before you play it.

If your instrument does not stay in tune, check these suggestions:
1 Be sure line is securely tied around taped part of eyebolt.
2 If tape touches wood, remove eyebolt and take off some tape.
3 Remove line and set eyebolt further into wood.
4 Brace box harp with two strips of wood, as shown.

If you are not sure of your tuning, have someone who is a musician check it with you.

Playing Chords on the Box Harp

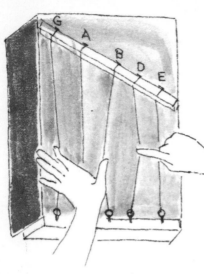

To make a chord, play three sounds together. Play as shown, unless your fingers are long enough to play three strings with one hand.

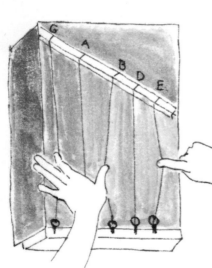

Try this chord next. You'll need extra long fingers to play this chord with one hand.

Repeat the first chord. Make up a song using these chords.

Choose a melody you know, such as "Are You Sleeping?", and play these chords as you sing.

First, practice plucking in the rhythm indicated. The strings on the top line are plucked by the right hand. The **B** and **G** strings below are plucked together by the left hand.

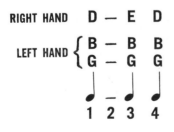

RIGHT HAND   D — E   D

LEFT HAND   { B — B   B
           G — G   G

1   2   3   4

Playing the Box Harp as You Sing "Are You Sleeping?"

Here is how the chords fit with the song. Ask a drummer to tap a 4–beat pattern as you play and sing.

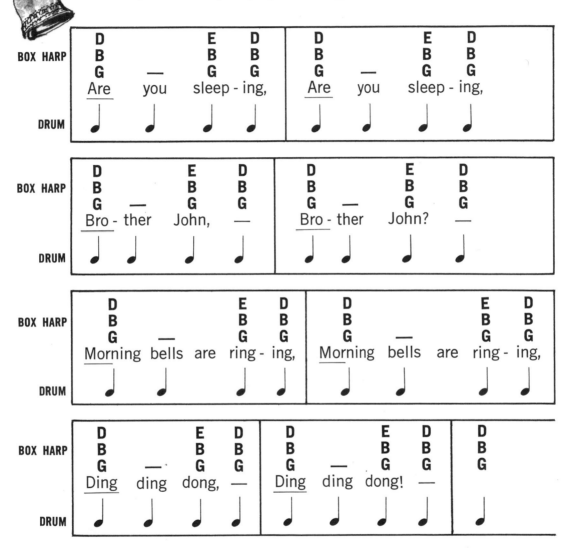

73

Steal Away

Here is a spiritual for you to try on your box harp. Have a drummer tap a 2-beat pattern throughout the piece. Notice how the words fit with the drum pattern. First say the words to learn the rhythm of the song, then pluck the strings as marked for the melody.

The small letters **g, a, b, d, e** indicate a very light pluck to help you mark a hold. When you have the feeling of the holds, shake your hand to the side instead of plucking the small letters.

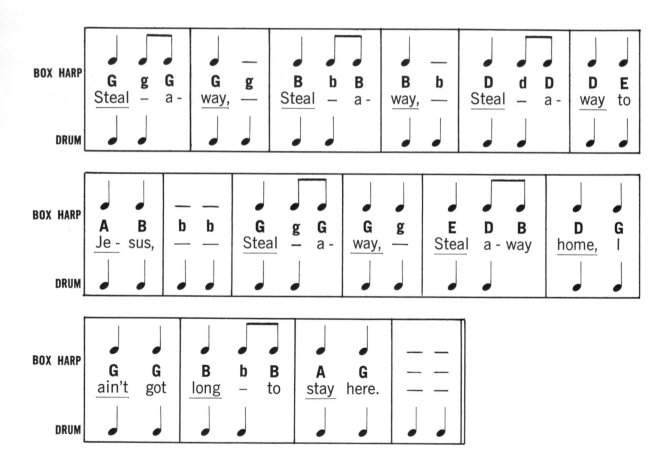

Sing as you play. See if you can make the melody sound natural and expressive while keeping the basic pulse of the song.

74

A Ten-Stringed Harp

You can make a box harp with ten strings and tune the strings to your xylophone: G_1, A_1, B_1, D_1, E_1, G_2, A_2, B_2, D_2, E_2. These same pitches can be found on a piano. Use **G, A, B, D, E** above middle **C** for the high pentatonic scale and **G, A, B** below middle **C**, and **D, E** for the low scale.

The larger box harp is made like the five-string harp. Use a box about 36 inches long and monofilament line as described on page 67 for the low pentatonic scale.

You'll probably want to try 15–pound test line for the high penta–tonic scale and 20-pound test for the low scale.

Your box harp can also be tuned to the Japanese pentatonic scale, or you can use eight strings and tune to the major or minor scale with the help of your metallophone. The major scale is G_1, A_1, B_1, C_1, D_1, E_1, $F_1^{\sharp}$, G_1, and the minor scale is G_1, A_1, $B_1^{\flat}$, C_1, D_1, $E_1^{\flat}$, $F_1^{\sharp}$, G_1.

Playing the Ten-Stringed Harp

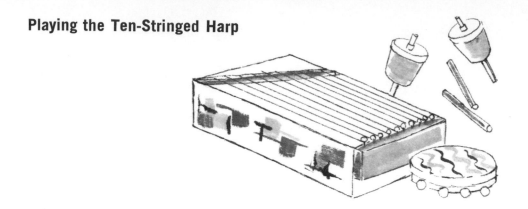

This melody can be played on your 10-string box harp or on your metallophone or xylophone. Use D_1, G_2, A_2, B_2, D_2, E_2. Have some rhythm players begin with the rhythm of the melody. The second time round, play the melody.

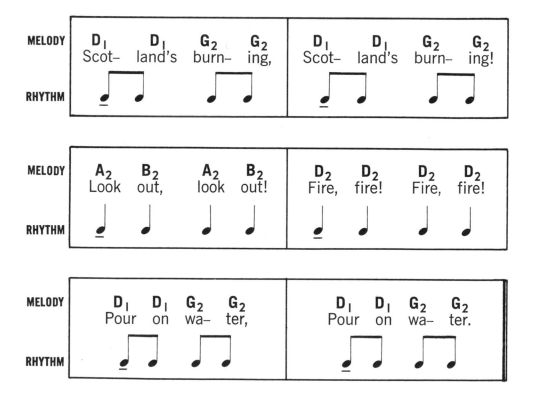

Guitars Big and Small

You can make a single–string instrument to strum like a guitar or play like a violin or cello with a bow. You will need a milk carton and a stick about 1 or 2 inches wide and 1/4 to 3/8 inch thick. Lattice or wooden lath are about right for this.

For a small guitar or violin use a half–gallon carton and a stick about 15 inches long. You will need 20–pound test monofilament line and an eyebolt, size 1/4x2.

A gallon carton, a stick 24 inches long, and 30–pound test mono-filament line will make a big guitar or cello. It also needs an eyebolt.

Your tools are a saw, a serrated kitchen knife wound with friction tape or a razor blade in a holder, a ball point or felt tip pen, and a 7/32–inch bit and drill.

Cut a groove 1/2 inch deep at one end of the stick. Drill a hole about 1/2 inch from the other end of the stick for the eyebolt.

  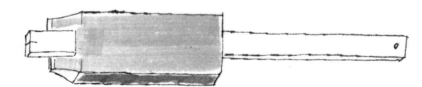

Cut slots in the milk carton at top and bottom about 1/2 inch from the edge, as shown, to fit the stick. If you wind a small serrated kitchen knife with friction tape to leave only a short part free, you have a safe tool. Wedge the carton in a wastebasket (do NOT hold it in your arms) while cutting. Slip the stick through the slots.

Wrap friction tape around the eyebolt, as shown. Tie a matchstick to one end of the monofilament line.

Slip the line through the groove in the stick, using the matchstick to keep it from sliding out. Carry the line over the top of the carton to the eyebolt and wrap it clockwise around the tape, then tie it. By turning the eyebolt clockwise you can tighten the line.

To make a bridge for your instrument, cut a piece of cardboard about 3 inches long and 1 inch wide. Score it (cut it just enough to bend easily) and tape it as illustrated.

Place the bridge under the line, and your guitar is ready to tune. If you have no drill, make a slot in the other end of the stick. Loop the string over the slot. If the line is too loose, remove it and make loops around the matchstick, as shown. You will then have to adjust the tuning of the string by moving the bridge until the string is at the correct pitch.

Tuning Your Guitar

Tune the guitar made from the half-gallon milk carton to the G_I pipe of your metallophone or to the **G** above middle **C** on a piano. You can also use the **G** of a pitch pipe.

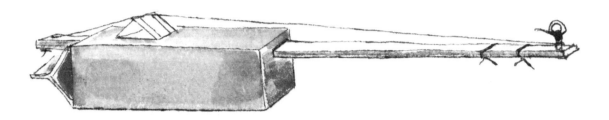

Once your string is tuned to G_I, try to find the A_I of your metallophone on your small guitar. Press your finger against the string about an inch away from the bolt end. When the sound of the string matches the A_I, mark that spot with a pencil.

Tie string with a slip knot around the neck of your guitar, as shown. Position the string for pitch A_I and pull the knot tight. This will be a guide for your finger when you want to find this pitch. Find the B_I pitch in the same way and tie a second string there.

Be sure to tune your string to G_I whenever you begin to play your guitar. It will slip out of pitch when not in use.

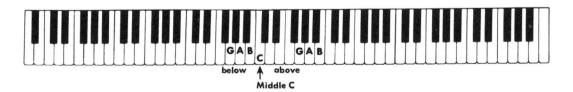

Tune a guitar made from the gallon carton to the **G, A,** and **B** below middle **C** on a piano.

At Your Door I'm Knocking

Here is a French folk song to play on your guitar. Be sure to press your finger firmly against the string at the place marked **A** when you want the **A** sound. Move your finger to the place marked **B** when you want the **B** sound. This song follows a 4-beat pattern. Let the drummer beat the pattern to help you keep the rhythm of the song.

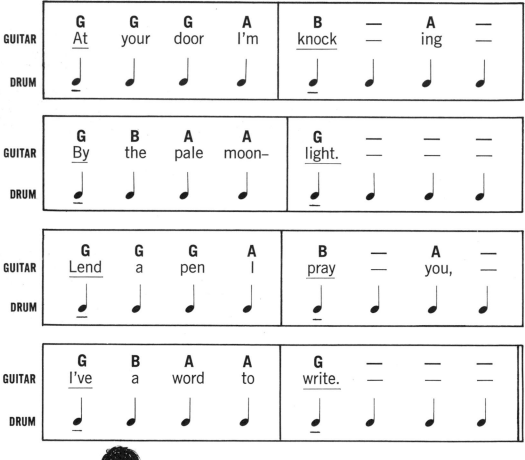

A Javanese Children's Song

Use your one-string guitar and drum to accompany this Javanese children's song. The melody will sound pleasant on the metallophone or xylophone.

The drummer sets up a 2-beat pattern and is followed by the guitar player, who keeps the drummer's rhythm. Before the guitar player begins, he should find the D_1 sound on the guitar and mark it with a fret. The metallophone or xylophone player performs the melody in a steady running rhythm after the first walking tap. This player should practice his part slowly with a drummer.

After you are familiar with the melody, try other accompaniment variations on your guitar.

Dragonfly

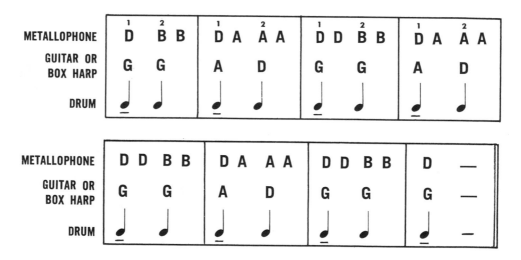

The song "Dragonfly" is from <u>Music in Java</u> by J. Kunst and is used with permission of the publishers, Martinus Nijhoff, The Hague, Netherlands. It is transposed from the original key.

Making a Violin Bow

Turning your little or big guitar into a violin or cello is really quite simple. All you need is a bow.

Find a stick, preferably green and about as big around as a pencil; cotton sewing thread; masking tape. You will need some rosin, and you can buy this at a music store for about fifty cents. A piece lasts a long time.

Cut the stick about 30 inches long and trim it neatly. Wind tape about 4 inches from the heavy end and also around the lighter end of the stick, as shown. Use several layers of tape.

Tie the cotton thread at the small end and then pull gently to form a slight bow in the stick.

Wrap at least 30 strands of thread back and forth around the bow, as illustrated. Tie the thread securely. Apply rosin and your bow is ready.

Playing Your Violin

Try out your violin. Hold your instrument as shown and draw the bow back and forth across the string in a steady marching rhythm. To get a good sound, use a little pressure as you draw the bow.

When you have learned to bow, practice bowing with your finger pressed down for the **A** sound and the **B** sound. When you can play these notes clearly, you are ready to try your guitar song "At Your Door I'm Knocking" on your violin.

How Old Are You, My Pretty Little Miss?

Try a melody of your own with three notes. Here is a way to work out a melody. First clap a short rhythm. Use this rhythm for the first part of your melody. Does it sound like a question? Then clap an answering rhythm. Use that for the second part of your melody. Here is an example.

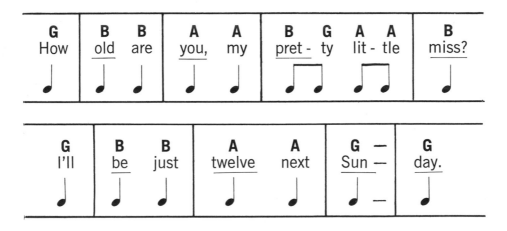

G	B	B	A	A	B	G	A	A	B
How	old	are	you,	my	pret -	ty	lit -	tle	miss?

G	B	B	A	A	G —	G
I'll	be	just	twelve	next	Sun —	day.

Try very slow music on your violin, using long slow bowing. Try gay music, using quick bowing.

84

A Double Bass from a Carton

If you want a stringed instrument with a deep tone, like a double bass in an orchestra, here is a simple way to make one.

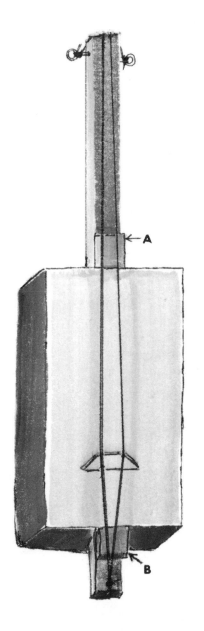

Find a large cardboard carton, about 31x20x15 inches. Tape closed.

Get a piece of wood 1 or 2 inches wide and 4 feet long. Drill holes at each end, using a 7/32-inch bit. Cut slots in the ends of the carton to fit the wood snugly. The slots should be 1–1/2 inches from the edge. Turn to page 77 for safety suggestions.

Slide the stick through the box so that it extends about 6 inches at the bottom. Hold the stick in place by gluing and taping two blocks, marked A and B in the illustration.

Use heavy or twisted monofilament line for the string and a light piece of wood for the bridge.

Insert eyebolts and tighten strings to play. Attach bridge, and tune to the second **G** below middle **C** on a piano and to the **D** above this **G.**

A String Concert

You can play your melody "At Your Door I'm Knocking" as a trio, or group of three players. One member plays the melody and the other two members play an accompaniment. Have your drummer play a slow 4-beat pattern to help you stay together.

Before you begin, be sure all of the **G**'s are in tune with one another.

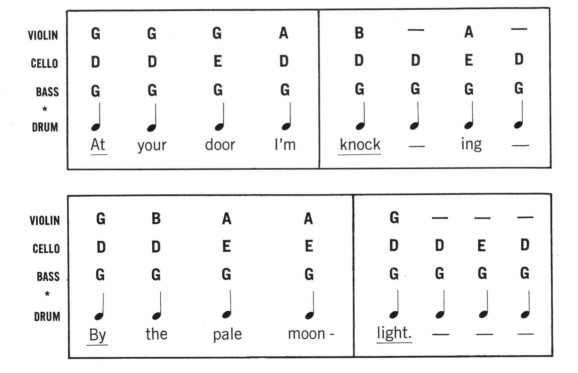

VIOLIN	G	G	G	A	B	—	A	—
CELLO	D	D	E	D	D	D	E	D
BASS	G	G	G	G	G	G	G	G
* DRUM	♩	♩	♩	♩	♩	♩	♩	♩
	At	your	door	I'm	knock	—	ing	—

VIOLIN	G	B	A	A	G	—	—	—
CELLO	D	D	E	E	D	D	E	D
BASS	G	G	G	G	G	G	G	G
* DRUM	♩	♩	♩	♩	♩	♩	♩	♩
	By	the	pale	moon -	light.	—	—	—

All Together!

By now you and your friends have enough different instruments for many kinds of playing together. Here is one way to combine the sounds you can make into music.

Have your string players join you while you play the melody of "Dragonfly," the Javanese children's song, on the metallophone. Make your song grow by adding a second melody, shown below, for the panpipes or harp.

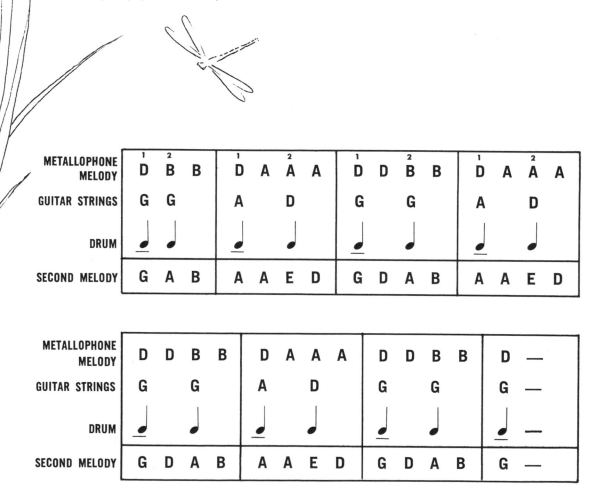

Swing Low, Sweet Chariot

Bring all your instruments together to play "Swing Low, Sweet Chariot." Choose a conductor to keep all the players together. It is the conductor's job to conduct the beat pattern of the song.

For this song, the pattern is four beats. One drummer should play the four beats on his drum, and another drummer should play the rhythmic pattern of the words on his drum. This will help everyone stay together.

Learn the melody. It can be played on the metallophone or xylophone. Remember that the small letters, **g, a, b, d, e,** mark holds. Tap the holds lightly or give a shake of the hand to the side.

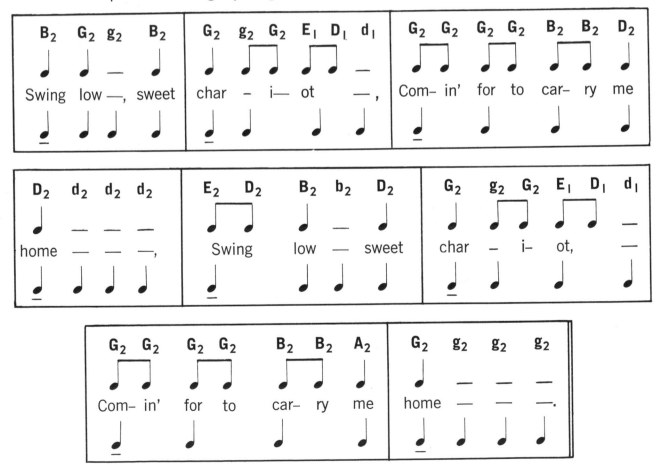

You can accompany the melody with a very simple repeated pattern. Find friends to play your other instruments while you play the melody. They should keep the rhythm of the 4-beat pattern of the drums.

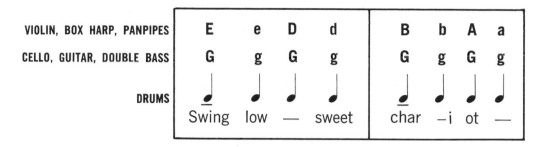

VIOLIN, BOX HARP, PANPIPES	E	e	D	d		B	b	A	a
CELLO, GUITAR, DOUBLE BASS	G	g	G	g		G	g	G	g
DRUMS	♩	♩	♩	♩		♩	♩	♩	♩
	Swing	low	—	sweet		char	–i	ot	—

You probably know verses for "Swing Low, Sweet Chariot." Sing them and see if you can find the tune on your metallophone or other melody instruments.

I looked over Jordan, and what did I see,
Comin' for to carry me home?
A band of angels comin' after me,
Comin' for to carry me home!

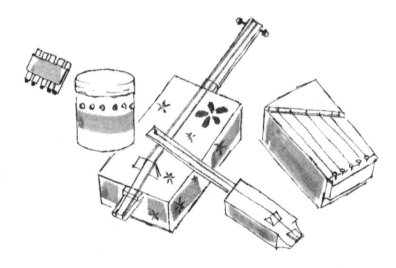

A Voyage to Outer Space

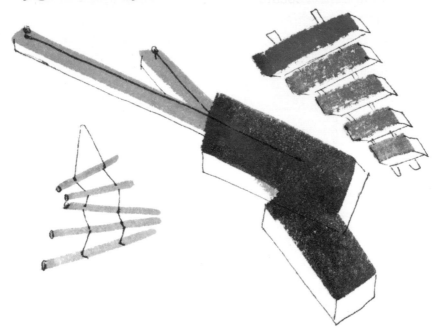

Making music together can lead on to many new ideas. Suppose that you bring all your instruments and players together and create your own music for a drama in movement.

How can you begin? Think of a theme, such as "Voyage into Outer Space." Think of movements that dramatize your theme and find friends to help you in planning. Experiment with how you think the movements should be, then begin to put music with the action.

Be sure to try unusual sounds on your instruments. You can slide up and down the metallophone or xylophone, for example, and have an interesting sound. Try this on your single-string instruments, too. Pluck the string as you slide your finger along it. This may sound most effective on the big double bass. Jangle your curtain-rod metallophones. For another unusual sound, find a piece of pipe and raise and lower it in a bucket of water as you tap it.

Sounds like these are ones you may want to use in your outer-space music to add a sense of mystery to your voyage into the unknown.

A MORE ADVANCED INSTRUMENT If you are ambitious, you might like to try making a guitar entirely of wood, custom made to fit your size.

A Guitar Made of Wood

Here Are the Materials You Will Need:

Either 1/8- or 3/16-inch plywood paneling, available in 4x7 panels.

If you can get scraps from the lumberyard, so much the better.

Two 1x2-inch wood strips, one 20 inches long and one 15 inches long.

One ¼x2-inch wood strip, 24 inches long. Lattice is ¼-inch thick.

Small scraps of wood.

Guitar keys and strings, purchased from music store.

White glue, a few nails.

Here Are the Tools You Will Need:

With the keyhole saw, cut a piece of 1/8-inch plywood about 4 feet long and 3 or 4 inches wide. First, lay the panel flat on a table. Weight the panel down. Draw a line to follow. Hold the saw firmly, but saw slowly and with ease.

Soak the plywood in water overnight to make it pliable.

Slowly bend plywood into a bow shape and clamp to 20-inch long wood strip using the C-clamp. Nail in place with nails you can clinch.

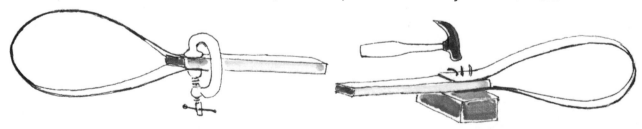

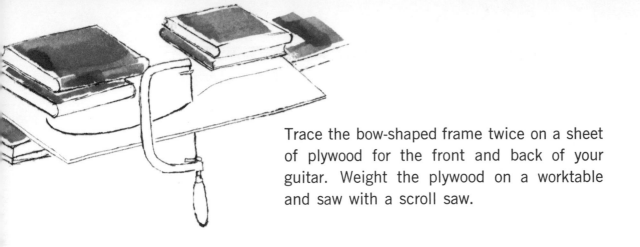

Trace the bow-shaped frame twice on a sheet of plywood for the front and back of your guitar. Weight the plywood on a worktable and saw with a scroll saw.

Cut a sound hole in the front panel with the scroll saw. Drill a hole first. Take the blade from the saw, put it through the hole, then back on the saw. Cut. A keyhole saw can be used.

Make a bridge, as shown, and glue and brad to the front panel. Drill six holes, 1/2 inch apart.

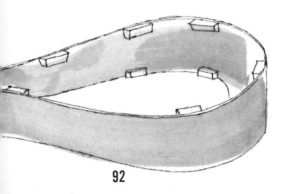

Glue small pieces of wood flush with the top and bottom edges of the frame. These will help hold the front and back panels in place. Let dry.

Glue front and back panels to frame. Weight with books until dry.

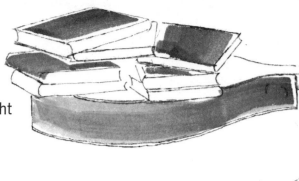

Use the 1/4x2-inch strip for the fingerboard. Glue and hold in place with brads. This will have the frets.

Saw a 15-inch strip of 1x2 wood in two pieces, as shown. Glue on either side of the neck of the guitar to make the pegbox.

For a few dollars you can buy a set of guitar keys where guitars are sold and repaired. Drill holes in the pegbox to fit the keys and mount them.

Use regular guitar strings and string from bridge to pegbox.

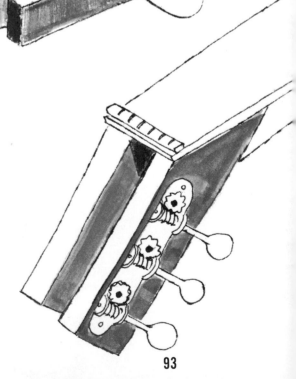

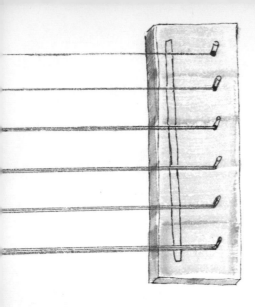

If the strings do not have knobs on the ends, tie knots. Use matchsticks for hole plugs on the bridge, as shown. Your homemade guitar is strung just as a purchased one is.

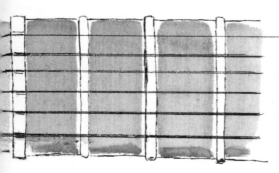

Tune your guitar to a piano or pitch pipe. Glue matchsticks for frets, following the diagram in a guitar book and using the piano to find the positions. Put on just the frets you will use.

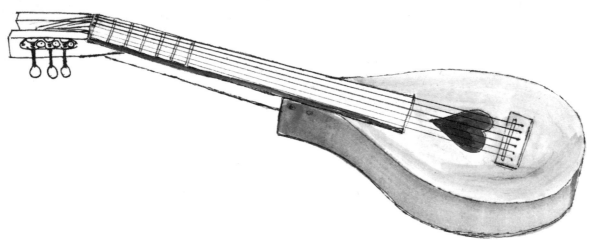

A guitar instruction book will give you helpful directions about playing your guitar. Of course it will help if you know someone who plays a guitar well enough to show you how to begin.

A Wooden Harp

You can make a durable, better sounding harp from wood. Use 1/8–inch plywood and strips 1x2, 1x3, or 1x4 for the sound box. Scrap wall paneling from a lumberyard will do. Saw plywood as shown in Picture 1. Cut frame strips and glue to bottom panel, Picture 2. Glue (and nail if you wish) top in place. Weight with bricks or books and let dry.

Drill 10 holes through plywood and into frame, as in Picture 3. Make 10 grooves in wood strip (see page 68), and glue strip in place. Weight and let dry for one hour. Insert eyebolts wound with friction tape. String and tune harp as described on pages 71 and 75. Refer to page 67 for information about monofilament line.

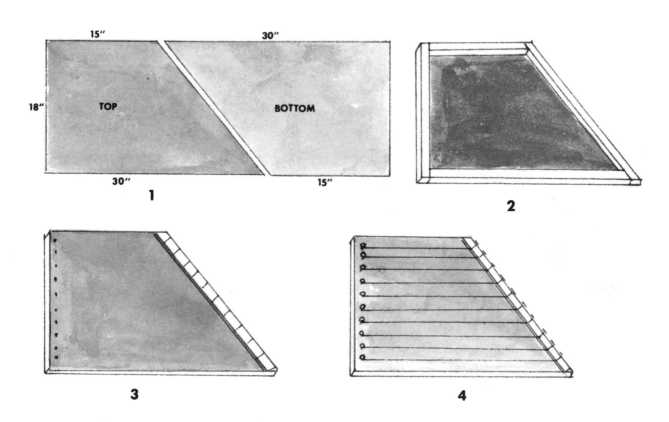

Music Involvement Series

Book One MUSIC AND INSTRUMENTS FOR CHILDREN TO MAKE
Book Two RHYTHMS, MUSIC AND INSTRUMENTS TO MAKE

Children are naturally creative, John Hawkinson believes, and this creativity grows as children learn techniques for using art and craft materials. To put theory into practice, John Hawkinson has written and illustrated books that show how to work with water colors, pastels, and nature materials. When girls and boys see how they can use art and craft media, they freely supply their own original ideas and viewpoints.

Wondering if this same approach could be used for music, John Hawkinson went to Martha Faulhaber to discuss his ideas. Mrs. Faulhaber, who has graduate and undergraduate degrees in music, is a professional pianist and teacher. She teaches privately, but she has also had classroom experience. She has worked in the Head Start program and has taught at Dr. Bruno Bettelheim's Orthogenic School at the University of Chicago. She has studied in France and in this country under the pianist Rudolph Ganz. Electronic music and modern music theory are two fields in which Mrs. Faulhaber is studying at DePaul University, Chicago.

Always working out their ideas with children, Mr. Hawkinson and Mrs. Faulhaber began writing the kind of book they hoped would embody a free, experimental introduction to music. The result has been a exciting project that has led to two books and to tape recordings and films. While Mrs. Faulhaber has contributed theory and basic musical concepts, Mr. Hawkinson has worked out the construction details for the musical instruments and created illustrations for each activity.